PRIMITIVE EXPERIENCES
OF LOSS

PRIMITIVE EXPERIENCES OF LOSS

Working with the Paranoid–Schizoid Patient

Robert T. Waska

KARNAC

LONDON   NEW YORK

Extracts from "Notes on Some Schizoid Mechanisms", from *Envy and Gratitude and Other Works*, by Melanie Klein, published by Hogarth Press, 1975, reprinted by permission of the Random House Group.

PRIMITIVE EXPERIENCES
OF LOSS

PRIMITIVE EXPERIENCES OF LOSS
Working with the
Paranoid–Schizoid Patient

Robert T. Waska

KARNAC
LONDON   NEW YORK

First published in 2002 by
H. Karnac (Books) Ltd.
6 Pembroke Buildings, London NW10 6RE
A subsidiary of Other Press LLC, New York

British Library Cataloguing in Publication Data
A C.I.P. for this book is available from the British Library

ISBN: 1 85575 260 3

10 9 8 7 6 5 4 3 2 1

Edited, designed, and produced by Communication Crafts

www.karnacbooks.com

Printed and bound by Antony Rowe Ltd, Eastbourne

CONTENTS

v

PREFACE

I have gradually become aware, when working from a psychoanalytic perspective, of the impact and primacy of loss in many patients' life histories. While these patients have usually suffered external trauma, neglect, and loss in their childhoods, my clinical focus is on the deeply imbedded and self-perpetuating nature of intrapsychic loss.

The patients who most exhibit these problems are diagnostically within what Melanie Klein has termed the paranoid–schizoid position. In this developmental position, projective identification is a psychological cornerstone in how the ego relates to and organizes internal experience. This dynamic is explained in detail in the Introduction, in which I review Klein's concept of the paranoid–schizoid stance and its associated defences.

Part one of the book looks at the contributions of the symbol function and projective identification. Symbolism is an integral part of psychic growth and integration. It fosters trust in sustainable and resilient object relations. Primitive, paranoid–schizoid experiences of loss tend to prevent or destroy symbolic functioning and its associated whole-object potentials. Chapter one describes these concepts from a theoretical standpoint.

Chapter two illustrates through detailed clinical material the theoretical idea of a primitive internal state of loss. The desperate and overwhelming phantasies and anxieties so common with these patients are brought to life with moment-to-moment clinical data.

Chapter three uses further case reports to show the particular moments in which the patient's object shifts from a more idealized, nourishing helper to a demonized foe. Narcissistic defences and projective identification are over-utilized to shore up the paranoid ego; however, this strategy actually leaves the ego more vulnerable to these phantasies of loss and persecution.

Chapters four and five show how dreams, and the patient's unique way of sharing dreams with the analyst, lead to a better understanding of the paranoid–schizoid experience of loss. Dreams can be remarkably clear in demonstrating the pivotal point at which the ego feels betrayed, attacked, and annihilated.

Chapter five describes several patients who tried their best to escape the persecution and isolation of loss by disconnecting from the analyst and other important objects. By sabotaging their own thinking processes and denying difference in favour of manic union and sameness, they try to reassure themselves magically. This idealized union is brittle and proves difficult to maintain. Ultimately, this defence promotes an increased sense of potential loss, rejection, and persecution.

Chapters six and seven follow in depth the cases of two patients. In the exploration of the here-and-now transference dynamic, several points emerge. Paranoid–schizoid patients who are struggling with more catastrophic versions of loss often fall into two camps. The first involves an aggressive, narcissistic transference in which envy and splitting are prominent. In the other, the transference state is much more masochistic and quietly demanding. While at first glance the latter can appear to be indicative of a higher functioning, depressive patient, the clinical material reveals the same underlying sense of fragmentation and hopeless, anxious dread of annihilation.

Part two is an in-depth study of the more masochistic profile mentioned previously. Melanie Klein's developmental views are described in chapter eight, along with examination of the concept of paranoid–schizoid guilt. These theoretical points are given form with the extensive case material presented in chapter nine.

Chapter ten addresses the specific transference and counter-transference situations that tend to arise with masochistic patients who are fending off primitive loss. One particular transference problem—grievance—is described in chapter eleven. Grievance toward the object can become the primary vehicle for the feelings and defences concerning loss. The patient's feelings regarding rejection, attack, and complete breakdown of safety or emotional nourishment are also examined, as they are funnelled through the phantasy and transference of grievance.

In the final chapter, I gather together all these ideas and convey the essence of what loss is within the paranoid–schizoid experience. The lack of forgiveness, repair, restitution, or understanding in this dark internal world leaves the ego in a state of perpetual danger and despair. Throughout the book the clinical material shows how psychotic, borderline, and masochistic patients can be entombed in a paranoid–schizoid phantasy of primitive loss, in which desperately sought-after idealized good objects turn into abandoning, attacking, bad objects. Loss of the good object brings with it annihilation of the self. Pathological reliance on projective identification, splitting, masochism, and manic defences rigidifies a cycle of idealization, greed, envy, loss, and persecution. If the analyst can focus on these elements in the transference as well as on the ongoing phantasies of idealization–oral aggression–loss–persecution, then these pathological cycles can gradually change.

PRIMITIVE EXPERIENCES
OF LOSS

Introduction

The focus of this book is on the paranoid–schizoid patient's experience of loss, abandonment, and persecution. These primitive patients show up regularly in our consulting offices and offer difficult clinical challenges. Stormy and confusing treatment situations unfold, with transferences involving loss, annihilation anxiety, and persecution. Many of these paranoid–schizoid patients cope with these fears and feelings of envy by erecting masochistic defences. Masochistic submission and paranoid struggles for control and recognition mask hostility and loss.

Melanie Klein wrote extensively on the roles of loss, phantasy, and anxiety. However, Klein and her followers place most of their emphasis on loss within the depressive position. I explore the ego's experience of loss in the paranoid–schizoid position and the way projective identification is then used to cope with overwhelming anxieties of annihilation and separation. I also explore the role of early precursors to symbolic function and the impact of symbolization on intrapsychic loss, both within the paranoid–schizoid position.

Projective identification (PI) is a primary defence in the paranoid–schizoid position and it figures prominently in how the ego

1

copes with primitive experiences of loss. Symbolism seems to play a role in the dynamics between the paranoid–schizoid position, phantasies of loss, and the mechanism of PI.

I feel that it is critical in all analytic treatments to show and explain to patients, through interpretation, how they are experiencing loss in the transference relationship. In a similar manner, I illustrate my work here with abundant case material.

The paranoid–schizoid position

To explore the issues of primitive loss within the paranoid–schizoid position, I start by summarizing Melanie Klein's discovery of the paranoid–schizoid concept and how it is defined in Kleinian circles. In addition, reviewing Klein's views of the ego, the object, and PI is helpful.

Melanie Klein introduced the concept of the paranoid–schizoid position in 1946. She had certainly discovered much of her theory before, but it really crystallized in her paper, "Notes on Some Schizoid Mechanisms". After this paper she refined her ideas, and Kleinians have found it a crucial tool in their day-to-day clinical work with regressed and disturbed patients.

Klein (1946) summarized her findings by stating that

> In the first few months of life anxiety is predominantly experienced as fear of persecution and that this contributes to certain mechanisms and defences which characterize the paranoid and schizoid positions. . . . These mechanisms and defences are part of normal development and at the same time form the basis for later schizophrenic illness. [p. 22]

She then stated more fully:

> I have often expressed my view that object relations exist from the beginning of life, the first object being the mother's breast which is split into a good (gratifying) and bad (frustrating) breast; this splitting results in a division between love and hate. I have further suggested that the relation to the first object implies its introjection and projection, and thus from the beginning object relations are moulded by an interaction be-

tween introjection and projection, between internal and external objects and situations. These processes participate in the
building up of the ego and super-ego and prepare the ground
for the onset of the Oedipus complex in the second half of the
first year.

From the beginning the destructive impulse is turned
against the object and is first expressed in phantasied oral-
sadistic attacks on the mother's breast which soon develop into
onslaughts on her body by all sadistic means. The persecutory
fears arising from the infant's oral-sadistic impulses to rob
the mother's body of its good contents, and the anal-sadistic
impulses to put his excrements into her (including the desire
to enter her body in order to control her from within), are of
great importance for the development of paranoia and schizophrenia. . . . This early period I described as the "persecutory
phase" or rather "paranoid position" as I termed it later. I thus
held that preceding the depressive position there is a paranoid
position. If persecutory fears are very strong, and for this reason as well as others the infant cannot work through the paranoid position, then the working through of the depressive
position is in turn impeded.

. . . Some fluctuations between the schizoid and the
depressive position always occur and are part of normal development. No clear division between the two stages of
development can therefore be drawn, because modification is
a gradual process and the phenomena of the two positions
remain for some time to some extent intermingled and interacting. In abnormal development this interaction influences, I
think, the clinical picture both of some forms of schizophrenia
and of manic-depressive illness. [p. 22]

Hanna Segal (1974) has been a primary developer of Klein's
thinking. Regarding the paranoid–schizoid position, she states:

quite early, the ego has a relationship to two objects; the primary object, the breast, being at this stage split into two parts,
the ideal breast and the persecutory one. The phantasy of the
ideal object merges with, and is confirmed by, gratifying experiences of love and feeding by the real external mother, while
the phantasy of persecution similarly merges with real experiences of deprivation and pain, which are attributed by the
infant to the persecutory objects. Gratification, therefore, not
only fulfils the need for comfort, love and nourishment, but is

also needed to keep terrifying persecution at bay; and deprivation becomes not merely a lack of gratification, but a threat of
annihilation by persecutors. The infant's aim is to try to acquire, to keep inside and to identify with the ideal object, seen
as life-giving and protective, and to keep out the bad object
and those parts of the self which contain the death instinct. The
leading anxiety in the paranoid–schizoid position is that the
persecutory object or objects will get inside the ego and overwhelm and annihilate both the ideal object and the self. These
features of the anxiety and object-relationships experienced
during this phase of development led Melanie Klein to call it
the paranoid–schizoid position, since the leading anxiety is
paranoid, and the state of the ego and its objects is characterized by the splitting, which is schizoid. [p. 26]

Segal (1974) goes on to clarify:

It has to be remembered that a normal infant does not spend
most of his time in a state of anxiety. On the contrary, in favourable circumstances, he spends most of his time sleeping,
feeding, experiencing real or hallucinatory pleasures and thus
gradually assimilating his ideal object and integrating his ego.
But all infants have periods of anxiety, and the anxieties and
defences which are the nucleus of the paranoid–schizoid position are a normal part of human development. [p. 35]

Finally, Schafer (1997) has summarized some of these ideas:

In the paranoid–schizoid position the focus is very much on aggression or self and other directed destructiveness, much of it
in the form of envy and fear of envy, and on grandiosity, while
in the depressive position the focus is on love, understanding,
concern, reparation, desire, and various other forms of regard
for the object as well as on destructiveness and guilt. The paranoid–schizoid position is also characterized by typical defenses
such as splitting and projective identification; the depressive
position, by regression (to the paranoid–schizoid position),
flight to a manic position featuring denial and idealization of
self and other, or bondage to a reparative position relative to
the imagined damaged objects. Mature functioning rests on
one's having attained an advanced phase of the depressive
position in which object love and sublimatory activity are relatively stable; however, regressive pulls are never absent. [p. 4]

The ego

Regarding the ego, Melanie Klein embraced Freudian thoughts. However, she developed a distinct emphasis of her own. She felt that the ego existed from birth and was built up in complexity by introjecting the good object: the mother's breast. The good breast becomes the focal point for ego maturation. The good aspects of the mother fill the infant's inner world and become material for identification. These introjected objects and part-objects organize and fortify the ego and are constantly modified by other objects (St. Clair, 1986). Therefore, the ego is object-related from the beginning and is populated by multiple object relationships that constantly modify not only the ego but each other.

Klein (1959) wrote:

> The ego, according to Freud, is the organized part of the self, constantly influenced by instinctual impulses but keeping them under control by repression; furthermore it directs all activities and establishes and maintains the relation to the external world. . . . My work has led me to assume that the ego exists and operates from birth onwards and that in addition to the functions mentioned above it has the important task of defending itself against anxiety stirred up by the struggle within and by influences from without. Furthermore it initiates a number of processes from which I shall first of all select introjection and projection. To the no less important process of splitting, that is to say dividing, impulses and objects I shall turn later. [p. 250]

Regarding the development and maturation of the ego, Klein (1948) wrote:

> during the period from three to six months considerable progress in the integration of the ego comes about. Important changes take place in the nature of the infant's object relations and of his introjective-processes. The infant perceives and introjects the mother increasingly as a complete person. . . . Although these processes are still primarily focused on the mother, the infant's relation to the father (and other people in the environment) undergoes similar changes and the father too becomes established in his mind as a whole person. [p. 35]

In 1952, Klein wrote about the functions of the ego. She stated:

> among its first activities are the defence against anxiety and the use of processes of introjection and projection. . . . More recently I defined the drive toward integration as another of the ego's primal functions . . . its derivation from the life instinct. [1952a, p. 57]

In 1957, Klein elaborated these ideas when she wrote:

> it is likely that the primordial anxiety, engendered by the threat of the death instinct within, might be the explanation why the ego is brought into activity from birth onwards. The ego is constantly protecting itself against the pain and tension to which anxiety gives rise, and therefore makes use of defences from the beginning of post-natal life. [p. 216]

Klein (1963) pointed out how the early ego is dominated by splitting mechanisms designed to protect itself from the dangers of the death instinct. At the same time, the drive towards integration increases as the ego introjects more of the good object. She felt (Klein, 1957) that the ego's primary function was to deal with the primordial anxiety engendered by the death instinct. However, certain other ego functions emerge as a result of the struggle between the life and death instincts: "one of these functions is gradual integration which stems from the life instinct and expresses itself in the capacity for love" (p. 191).

Klein felt that the infant projects both the death instinct and the life instinct outwards to the external object, the frustrating or gratifying breast. A fluctuation of introjection and projection, based on self-protection, creates the mix of ego and object at the core of the developing ego. The infant splits the destructive feelings, retaining one part and projecting the other part outward. Simultaneously, the infant splits the libido, with part of the libido projected outward and the rest retained within. The fragment of good feelings, which is kept in the ego, establishes a relationship with the ideal good object. During these stages of ego development, partial objects operate within a disorganized inner world. As these disjointed phantasies become integrated, the infant has less need for omnipotent control over the object. Accurate ego perception results from a decrease in projective and introjective mechanisms.

Hinshelwood (1991) reviewed and summarized Klein's principle ideas on the ego:

For Klein the ego exists at birth, has a boundary and identifies objects. It has certain functions of an exceedingly primitive kind—(i) separating "me" from "not-me"; (ii) discriminating good (pleasant sensations) from bad; (iii) phantasies of incorporating and expelling (introjection and projection); and (iv) the phantasy of the mating of pre-conceptions and realizations. . . .

The ego, at first, alternates between states of integration and disintegration . . . [The ego includes] phantasies it has of struggling with anxieties experienced in the course of its relations with objects, which, although they are perceived in the colours of the instincts, create a world of experiences, anxieties, loves, hates, and fears rather than states of discharge. The ego's struggle is to maintain its own integrity in the face of its painful experiences of objects that threaten annihilation.

At first, however, the ego is very unstable, and its earliest functions are desperate efforts to establish stability. Klein conceived of the ego's first act differently at different stages in her theoretical development:

(i) in 1932 the primary function of the ego was the deflection of the death instinct outwards towards an external object that is then feared as a persecutor, the mechanism of projection.

(ii) in 1935 Klein began to view the introjection of the good object as the founding of the ego; finally,

(iii) in 1957 she described the first ego-function as a form of splitting, the basis of the capacity for judgement, though initially of a very narcissistic kind. [pp. 284–286]

The object

During the late 1920s, Klein elaborated on her ideas about the infantile phantasies that the child develops about being full of body parts, people, and things. For Klein, these phantasies of internal presences began at birth. All experiences and relationships with significant others were taken into the ego for protection.

Mitchell (1981) writes: "phantasies and anxieties concerning the state of one's internal object world become the underlying basis, Klein was later to claim, for one's behavior, moods, and sense of self" (p. 376).

The question of where the object originates is important to Klein's thinking. She believed that objects are inherent in and created out of the drives, independent of real people in the external world. For Klein, the drives contain a priori images of the outside world, which the ego searches out, motivated by both love and hate. These inherent phantasies and innate knowledge of the world include both part-object and whole-object encoded information at an unconscious level.

Perlow (1995) writes:

undoubtedly, it was the work of Melanie Klein that put the concept of internal objects into the center of the conceptual map of psychoanalysis . . . we have seen the development of a number of aspects of Melanie Klein's concept of internal objects. The main ones have been: (1) Internal objects as body-phantasies. This refers both to the phantasy of another person (or part of a person) physically inside the individual's body and to the bodily sensations which are experienced as objects. (2) Internal objects as referring to all contents of the mind-phantasies, memories, and perceptions of objects. The higher-level cognitive contents are considered to be rooted in the deep unconscious levels at which internal objects are experienced concretely (as in #1). (3) Internal objects as deeply influenced by the instincts. This is especially important in relation to the death instinct, which gives rise to experiences of dangerous and annihilating internal objects. [p. 55]

Perlow continues:

the concept of internal objects has played an interesting role on the border between self and object in Melanie Klein's theory— that self-object differentiation is a complex process and not a one-time, clear cut achievement. Internal objects combine aspects of self and object—both by combining qualities of self with qualities of the object (loving, hating, angry, reposing, and so on) and by combining the basic feeling of "me-ness" with "not-me-ness". Melanie Klein considered there to be a developmental process in which the confusion of self with object was gradually sorted out, in the progress from the paranoid–schizoid to the depressive position. [p. 56]

Klein felt drives to be intrinsically paired with objects. St. Clair (1986) notes that, for Klein, "every urge and instinct is bound up with an object" (p. 39).

Finally, Hinshelwood (1991) summarizes Klein's ideas:

In Klein's framework, the object is a component in the mental representation of an instinct.

What is represented in unconscious phantasy is a relationship between the self and an object in which the object is motivated with certain impulses, good or bad, related to the instinctual drives—oral, anal, genital, etc.—of the subject. . . . At the outset, Klein believed, the infant exists in relation to objects that are primitively distinguished from the ego—there are object-relations from birth. [pp. 362–363]

Projective identification

Klein presents the term projective identification for the first time in her 1946 paper, "Notes on Some Schizoid Mechanisms". As it is the birth of the term and a summing up of her thinking about it at the time, it is quoted here at length,

In hallucinatory gratification, two interrelated processes take place: the omnipotent conjuring up of the ideal object and situation, and the equally omnipotent annihilation of the bad persecutory object and the painful situation. These processes are based on splitting both the object and the ego. . . . So far, in dealing with the persecutory fear, I have singled out the oral element. However, while the oral libido still has the lead, libidinal and aggressive impulses and phantasies from other sources come to the fore and lead to a confluence of oral, urethral and anal desires, both libidinal and aggressive. Also the attacks on the mother's breast develop into attacks of a similar nature on her body, which comes to be felt as it was as an extension of the breast, even before the mother is conceived of as a complete person. The phantasied onslaughts on the mother follow two main lines: one is the predominately oral impulse to suck dry, bite up, scoop out and rob the mother's body of its good contents. . . . The other line of attack derives from the anal and urethral impulses and implies expelling dangerous substances (excrements) out of the self and into the mother. Together with these harmful excrements, expelled in hatred, split-off parts of the ego are also projected on to the mother or, as I would rather call it, into the mother. These excrements and bad parts of the self are meant not only to injure but also to control and to take possession of the object. In so far as the mother comes to contain the bad parts of the self, she is not felt to be a separate individual but is felt to be the bad self.

Much of the hatred against parts of the self is now directed toward the mother. This leads to a particular form of aggressive object-relation. I suggest of these processes the term *"projective identification"*. When projection is mainly derived from the infant's impulse to harm or to control the mother, he feels her to be a persecutor. . . . It is, however, not only the bad parts of the self which are expelled and projected, but also good parts of the self. Excrements then have the significance of gifts; and parts of the ego which, together with excrements, are expelled and projected into the other person represent the good, i.e. the loving parts of the self. The identification based on this type of projection again vitally influences object-relations. The projection of good feelings and good parts of the self into the mother is essential for the infant's ability to develop good object-relations and to integrate his ego. However, if this projective process is carried out excessively, good parts of the personality are felt to be lost, and in this way the mother becomes the ego-ideal; this process too results in weakening and impoverishing the ego. Very soon such processes extend to other people, and the result may be an over-strong dependence on these external representatives of one's own good parts. . . . The processes of splitting off parts of the self and projecting them into objects are thus of vital importance for normal development as well as for abnormal object-relations. [pp. 7–9]

The process of PI involves a phantasy of splitting off unacceptable parts of the self and sending them into another object as a protective and/or aggressive manoeuvre. Inner anxiety and danger are externalized and then managed in the outer world before reinternalizing them. Along with danger and hostility, loving feelings are also projected into the object as expressions of caring. Therefore, PI can produce cyclical anxieties as well as a sense of soothing, safety, and support.

So, for Klein, PI had different meanings and various clinical consequences. Locating aspects of the self in the object results in ego depletion and a weakened sense of identity. This is clinically significant and would require particular interpretations to restore the integrity of the ego. In 1957, Klein suggested that envy was often a factor in projective identification, representing the forced entry into another person in order to destroy that person's best qualities. This envy would push the person to use excessive PI, leading to a chronic depletion in the ego.

In 1952, Klein wrote:

> it seems that the processes underlying projective identification operate already in the earliest relation to the breast. . . . Accordingly, projective identification would start simultaneously with the greedy oral-sadistic introjection of the breast. This hypothesis is in keeping with the view often expressed by the writer that introjection and projection interact from the beginning of life. [1952c, p. 69]

Again in 1955, in a paper entitled "On Identification," Klein discussed the persecutory anxieties and splitting mechanisms that make up the intrapsychic context out of which PI arises (p. 143). Later in 1957, she points out that

> when things go wrong, excessive projective identification, by which split-off parts of the self are projected into the object, leads to a strong confusion between the self and the object, which also comes to stand for the self. Bound up with this is a weakening of the ego and a grave disturbance in object relations. [p. 192]

THE CONTRIBUTIONS OF PROJECTIVE IDENTIFICATION AND SYMBOLIZATION

Theoretical issues

"Even in the adult, the judgement of reality is never quite free
from the influence of [the] internal world."

Klein, 1959, p. 250

U nder certain circumstances, phantasies of past, current,
and impending loss can shade the intrapsychic world.
These fears and the repetitive defences that build up to
cope with these catastrophic anxieties shape internal and external
relationships. The ego forms internal bargains between itself and
the object in a desperate attempt to ward off the sense of self and
object loss.

As noted, the study of loss and separation within the paranoid–
schizoid experience has been rudimentary. Some Kleinians have
made mention of it, but they have made no extensive exploration.
Jean-Michel Quinodoz (1993) is an exception. His book does a re-
markable job of summarizing and exploring Kleinian views of
separation anxiety, and he does bring in the element of PI. I add to
his investigation by examining the specific unconscious dynamics
of loss within the paranoid–schizoid position.

While much has been written on the experience of loss within the depressive position, my emphasis here is on loss within the paranoid–schizoid position as well as the role of symbolic function and PI.

Anxieties concerning loss threaten the integrity of the ego and create a reliance on PI for protection. At the same time, excessive reliance on PI and splitting can foster even greater phantasies of loss and engender ego fragmentation. With many patients struggling with loss, the use of PI represents a significant portion of the moment-to-moment clinical work.

Klein described the ego as the mental agency accountable for not only instincts and the external world, but the countless anxieties created by the struggles with internal and external forces. To defend itself, the ego uses introjection and projection, mental mechanisms that operate in a reciprocal manner (Klein, 1959). Klein described the ego as constantly taking in of the outer world, its impact, its situations, and its objects. These introjections continually shape the ego. Through projection, the ego begins to re-shape the external world. The constant interplay of introjection and projection produce what we call personality and perception.

Hinshelwood (1991) writes:

> For Klein, introjected objects that are not identified with become internal objects, and she conceived of a varied and continuous process which populates the internal world with very many internal objects. This internal society becomes, on one hand, a resource of objects for identification and, on the other, a set of experiences about what the ego consists of and contains (good and bad). [p. 332]

Projective identification was a notion introduced by Klein in 1946 and involves the ongoing taking in and expelling of the infant's intrapsychic relationship with the world. It is an inner experience that simultaneously holds the expression of the internal world and the impression of the external world. The ego deposits certain feelings and aspects of the self into the object and remains in contact with that object. This connection is dynamic and involves a wide range of positive and negative feelings.

The patient's anxieties concerning love and hate for the object and the quest for knowledge about the object are all shaped by either paranoid–schizoid or depressive phantasies. These phantasies organize internal experience, which is contained, managed, and expressed through introjection and projective identification. The analysis of projective identification and its associated mechanisms is often the essence of a successful treatment. Rosenfeld (1983) writes: "in analytic work today the analysis of projective identification into the analyst and also into others in the patient's environment plays such a prominent part that we can no longer imagine how an analyst could work before 1946" (p. 262).

PI in the clinical setting

Issues of separation, loss, and PI are under-represented in verbatim clinical reports of Kleinian interpretations. However, Segal, Grotstein, and Spillius provide some examples of how PI looks in the clinical moment and how the analyst might react interpretatively.

Segal (1997c) reminds us that some PI situations are only understandable after the fact. Segal's patient had, as a child, lost her mother through a car accident. The patient's father had been the driver. When she began analysis, she could not drive. Once able to drive, she was propelled into a manic state. Segal writes:

> one day she gave me a rather frightening account of how recklessly she drove her motor bike. The next day, she missed the session without letting me know—which had never happened before. I was exceedingly anxious, and also guilty, wondering what I could have done to induce her to have an accident. The next day, she turned up, cool as a cucumber, and I was furious. I recognized, however, that she had inflicted on me an experience of her own, of waiting for her parents to return home, and being told of the accident. But that recognition came to me only after her return. In between, I had been dominated by her projections. [p. 112]

Here, Segal points to the countertransference aspects that so often figure in PI and the difficulty with interpreting PI as it occurs. Often it is only later that the analyst can translate to themselves what has occurred. Clearly, Segal experienced the patient's sense of loss through PI and her own countertransference. Only later could she bring it back to the patient in the form of an interpretation.

Grotstein (1986) feels that PI takes on many different forms, including an exchange of internal objects within the patient's phantasies. One patient began the hour by telling him how she didn't like a plant in his office. She added that she used to think of herself as a dismal gardener, but now she felt like she had a green thumb. Then she added that while she was making progress in her life, her analysis seemed to be totally stuck. Grotstein writes:

> I made the following interpretations: the weekend break caused you to feel that I had taken the good green breast with me for the weekend, leaving you with a barren and desolate backyard to cultivate. You then had a phantasy about entering into me, stealing my venture, possessing it for yourself, and identifying with it as the possessor of a "green thumb" which had no connection to me, and therefore you owed me no gratitude. At the same time, I am now believed to be the container of your undesired barren self which cannot make things grow. We have exchanged roles. [p. 182]

The patient told the analyst that she agreed, and she made associations in that direction, at first directly and then by displacement. Grotstein makes an immediate interpretation of PI and also is comfortable with analysing the deeper phantasy material. In addition, he makes use of body-part language. Here, he used all these elements to address the sense of loss, separation, and loneliness that the patient expressed through PI.

Spillius (1992) presents the case of "Mrs B" to illustrate PI in the clinical setting and states:

> this session was dramatic and painful—no question of maintaining my usual analytic stance on this day. In phantasy the patient was projecting a painful internal situation into me and acting in such a way as to get me to experience it while she got rid of it. [p. 66]

The patient had very high expectations of herself and was critical of herself when she fell short of them. She avoided these pressures by not aspiring too much and by blaming things on "fate".

Separations were difficult for her and she acted-out during breaks in the treatment. This session took place immediately before an unusually long break in the analysis. The patient was late for this particular session, and, after a long silence, Spillius commented that the patient seemed angry. After more silence, the patient began to complain about many things and said they were all petty complaints. Spillius tried to comment again, but the patient escalated into screaming and paranoid accusations. She felt that the analyst was deliberately not listening to her and was purposely distorting what she said. Spillius began to feel like a bad therapist. She writes:

> but I managed one small thought, which was that she must be feeling inadequate too, and that my leaving had a lot to do with it. Then came a second thought, that she hates herself for being cruel even though she gets excited by it. It felt to me as if I was like a damaged animal making her feel guilty, and she wanted to stamp me out. I said she couldn't bear for me to know how painfully attacking she is, how much she wants to hurt me, how cruel she feels; but she also can't stand it if I don't know, don't react. It means she is unimportant. [p. 67]

The patient screamed at her in response, telling her she was totally uninterested in what the analyst had said. After a long, tense silence, Spillius writes:

> what I said . . . was that I thought she felt I treated her cruelly, with complete scorn and indifference, as if she was boring and utterly uninteresting, and that was why I was leaving her. She felt that the only way she could really get this through to me was by making me suffer in the same way . . . I said she thought I was cruel for leaving her on her own so arbitrarily and that she therefore had a right to attack me in kind. But she also felt I was leaving her because she was so attacking. [p. 68]

Spillius explains the PI dynamics that held sway in thesession:

> My self doubt was, I believe, very similar to her feelings of unlovableness when her parent had left her. It was also very similar to the picture she painted of her parents, who had cruelly left her but felt very guilty and self-critical about it. Failure, damage, and imperfection were rampant in both of us. Her answer was to get the worst of it into me and then

attack and abandon me. She became the cruel me who was leaving her and the cruel parents who had left her, and I became the stupid, miserable child fit only for abandonment. [p. 69]

In 1994, Elizabeth Bott Spillius made a general statement about Kleinian technique that is important to consider as she is also noting the typical Kleinian approach to interpreting PI: "the basic features of Kleinian technique are . . . interpretation of anxiety and defence together rather than either on its own" (p. 348). We can see how this technical and theoretical tenet was used in the moment-to-moment analytic work of her previous 1992 case example. She addressed both the anxiety concerning loss and abandonment, as well as the patient's defences against it.

Annihilation

Klein (1955) felt that the infant's deepest fear is annihilation, as the result of the ego turning on itself. My view is that phantasies of losing the object produce a condition of dread and an implosive state of anxiety. The good object turns into a persecutory one that abandons the ego. The ego, overwhelmed by internal collapse, experiences annihilation. Segal (1981) writes: "Whenever the state of union with the ideal object is not fulfilled, what is experienced is not absence; the ego feels assailed by the counterpart of the good object—the bad object, or objects" [p. 51]. Therefore, for some patients, loss is the principle anxiety, followed by dread and persecution. They either fear losing their objects altogether, or fear losing the object's affective interest. This includes the loss of love, hate, and any other emotional notice. Anxieties regarding the maintenance of attachment fuel the patient's painful phantasies.

External trauma has often touched these patients at early stages of development. Klein (1957) writes: "another factor that influences development from the beginning is the variety of external experiences which the infant goes through" (p. 229). In 1959, she writes: "the importance of actual favourable and unfavourable experiences to which the infant is from the beginning subjected, first of all by his parents, and later on by other people [is of great significance]. External experiences are of paramount importance throughout life" (p. 256).

Unable to bear the destructive forces of the death instinct through a balance of good introjected objects, the early ego experiences a frustrating cycle of desperation and envy. Overwhelming internal chaos and violent confusion follow, which the ego projects into the object. The paranoid–schizoid experience is then of the object shifting from a good part-breast to an angry, abandoning part-breast that also attacks the ego. PI creates a negative-feedback loop in which the ego is attacked and deserted by the object and the ego begins to disintegrate and split more and more. This splitting process prevents the introjection of any potential good part-objects that could help bolster the shattered ego. In fact, anger and envy spoil these potential helpers and convert them into ever more cruel persecutory figures. A grim and hopeless impoverishment takes grip of the ego. Loss of hope and love and fear of desolation take over.

Ultimately, the infant's phantasies of loss relate to loss of the mother's body. Ogden (1984) writes: "phantasy content is always ultimately traceable to thoughts and feelings about the working and contents of one's own body in relation to the working and contents of the body of the other" (p. 501). Patients usually present with issues cloaked in much higher levels of mental discourse and use oedipal and pre-oedipal conflicts to shield this more core focus. Knowledge of one's own body and the body of the other produces various conflicts regarding love and hate. Loss of the mother's body is a fundamental dread that presides over more sophisticated states of mind and extends throughout the life-span.

Klein and her followers have elaborated on the fear of loss in the depressive position. The fears of hurting or even destroying the object bring on depressive anxieties, guilt, and remorse along with efforts at reparation. Manic defences help protect against these phantasies of having injured the whole object with one's ambivalent feelings.

Klein and her followers have also highlighted loss in the paranoid–schizoid position. Here, the threat is of annihilation. Restoration of the fallen object feels impossible and the ego is in danger of being destroyed. Destruction of the object seems final and signals the end of the ego's existence.

Experiences of loss

I wish to contribute to the understanding of loss in the paranoid–schizoid position by exploring the intrapsychic moment at which loss occurs and how the ego experiences this loss. When the all-good part-object shifts into multiple persecutory agents, twin feelings of loss overwhelm the ego. Love turns to hate, and hope turns to despair. The ego is simultaneously alone and under attack. The former helper, lover, mother, and extension of self turns into an enemy to be feared. It is a loss of innocence for the object and a loss of hope and love for the ego. This primitive state of abandonment and persecution is best understood by examining the ego's reliance on projective identification.

Placing the self into the object and introjecting aspects of that object are methods of denying separateness (Joseph, 1959; Klein, 1946) and therefore of eliminating the risk of separation and loss. While many patients may use PI to steal parts of the analyst or to spoil parts of the analyst that are intolerable, the patients I am highlighting are most concerned with maintaining attachment and preventing loss of the object. They often have greedy and envious phantasies and are bitter or rageful when not able to own the object. These feelings often occur parallel to and in defence against feelings of despair, fear, and abandonment. The inability to contact the ideal object combined with the phantasy of being attacked and betrayed by that object produces overwhelming anxiety and ego collapse. Projective identification is used in frantic, excessive, and aggressive ways to cope, usually only generating more of the same type of anxiety.

Loss can occur through transformation of good into bad (paranoid–schizoid anxiety) or through the ego's damaging of the object (depressive anxiety). Sometimes, when circumstances are such that the separations between self and object become painfully undeniable, a quick erasing of reality (paranoid–schizoid denial) or rationalization and selective attention (depressive intellectualization) are necessary.

Projective identification can serve to maintain an idealized object and save it from fragmentation. The ego feels frightened by the capacity to overwhelm an unavailable or weak object with greed and rage. By introjecting this object, the ego prevents loss. In introjection, the ego says "Come inside, I will save you from your weakness and my nasty attacks." Now the ego must expel any need, hunger, or frustration it has towards the object. Denial and projection of aggression or desire save the weak object. Yet, through projective identification, the ego now feels persecuted, manipulated, and ignored by outside forces. However, the ego has prevented loss through introjection and idealization of the threatened part-object.

If the ego feels its attacks and desires have overcome the object, PI is used to restore the object. By introjecting the injured object, the ego can then go about rebuilding and repairing its object. Loss is denied and culpability is negated. Through PI, the ego shifts feelings of loss into more tolerable phantasies. This type of PI process is also found in patients who feel they are so needy and poisonous that they will contaminate the analyst. They will identify with the damaged analyst and torture themselves in masochistic ways as a penance and a restorative act (Rosenfeld, 1983).

All these object-related concerns are primarily within the depressive position. However, loss is a factor in paranoid–schizoid anxieties as well. The difference is that part of the self is felt to be betraying another part of the self. The differentiation between ego and object is not as clear.

Betty Joseph (1959) wrote of a group of patients who exhibit marked repetition of maladaptive defences. They use excessive splitting and projective identification to master primitive anxieties. They are fearful of depending on the mother and on parts of her body. Patients whose primary unconscious phantasies concern loss of the object show similar unconscious repetitions. The ego's dependency, desire, and love trigger split-off feelings of envy, hatred, and resignation. These feelings threaten the object, and the ego feels capable of destroying what it needs the most. In the depressive position, this fosters anxieties regarding loss- and guilt-induced attempts at reparation. The ego begins to hide any need for or connection to the object.

However, in the paranoid–schizoid position, the acknowledgement of one's desires and urges stimulates the anxiety of complete object loss and subsequent loss of the self. Annihilation looms. Projective identification and introjection are defences used to prevent this loss and to prevent destruction of the much-needed and yearned-for good object. Excessive PI, used to eject anxieties concerning loss, leaves the ego barren and depleted. This makes the patient feel hollow and alone. Free association is difficult for these patients, as it is analogous with the life instinct and an interest or focus on one's objects. Therefore, these patients will violently resist exploration of their affects and phantasies. To investigate too deeply is to risk loss.

Hopefully, an infant and mother are involved in continuous projection and introjection of curiosity, love, need, and desire. This builds up a supply of good objects in the infantile ego and creates a beneficial cycle of taking in and giving love and concern. These good internal objects help detoxify the accumulation of hate, greed, envy, and pain. Attachment to reaffirming and supportive objects fills and fortifies the ego, which in turn shapes psychic structure.

Likierman (1993) writes:

> the infant projects what amounts to his entire loving capacity, as well as his capacity for pleasure, on to the object, and this is then introjected together with the object's actual goodness to become his very "core". It is thus of central importance to his existence. This makes clear Klein's belief that the good object is essential to sanity. [p. 249]

The accumulated hope between mother and child offsets moment-to-moment experiences of loss. The patients I am describing have had early and chronic negative experiences with their mother and often, later in life, with their fathers. Usually, these are a combination of cumulative internal, external, conscious, and unconscious situations. While often from divergent sources, multiple feelings of loss accumulate to form a basic threat of being separated from the body of the mother and from the blessing of her love.

These patients continue to use the tools of PI, splitting, and introjection in the clinical situation. Joseph (1985) writes:

> [what the patient brings in] can best be gauged by our focusing our attention on what is going on within the relationship, how he is using the analyst, alongside and beyond what he is saying. Much of our understanding of the transference comes through our understanding of how our patients act on us to feel things for many varied reasons; how they try to draw us

into their defensive systems; how they unconsciously act out with us in the transference, trying to get us to act out with them; how they convey aspects of their inner world built up from infancy . . . which we can often only capture through the feelings aroused in us, through our countertransference, used in the broad sense of the word. [p. 447]

The countertransference is often the best—and sometimes only—tool for detecting and understanding the nature of the PI processes occurring in the clinical moment.

Klein (1952c) felt that the ego constantly projects any terrifying internal situations into the external environment, creating a dangerous world filled with enemies. At the same time, introjection of real objects that are supportive and loving reduces anxiety and creates a sense of internal security. Projective identification is, in the optimum outcome, an ongoing interaction between the projection of sadistic and terrifying phantasies and the introjection of helpful and nurturing objects. This cycle gradually builds a balanced internal security system and trustful whole-object relationships. Therefore, the analysis of the transference must be the analysis of the PI and introjective mechanisms. Only through this process will the patient's internal experience become more in line with the reality of their lives.

The infantile ego is fragile and does not exhibit the full congruity of later maturation. This leads to a fluctuation between integration and disintegration (Klein, 1946). In the paranoid–schizoid position, the object is in parts or bits. If the ego feels that its desires and aggression have fragmented or torn apart the object, then (through introjection and PI) the ego will feel fragmented as well.

In 1948, Klein outlined her thoughts on anxiety and loss. She felt that the two main sources of anxiety regarding loss emerged from the complete dependence that the infant has on the mother. This reliance on the mother for tension reduction and gratification is "objective anxiety". The infant's fear that he or she has destroyed the mother with sadistic impulses creates "neurotic anxiety". Klein felt that there was a lifelong interaction between these two fears of loss. Internal and external factors constantly intertwine to make the infant fearful of losing the mother in a variety of ways. While Klein emphasized the depressive anxieties of harming the object, she also noted the fear of annihilation in the paranoid–

schizoid position. This was the result of the death instinct (1946). She also writes that

> other important sources of primary anxiety are the trauma of birth (separation anxiety) and frustration of bodily needs; and these experiences too are from the beginning felt as being caused by objects . . . they become through introjection internal persecutors and thus reinforce the fear of the destructive impulse within. [p. 5]

Part-objects and loss

My view is that in the paranoid–schizoid position the ego's hostility, frustration, and hunger bombard the good part-objects. These feelings occur when the ego feels threatened with separation from the ideal part-object. If these part-objects are not plentiful, cohesive, and able to withstand the ego's aggression, then they simultaneously perish and then return as bad objects seeking revenge. This is the intrapsychic sequence of loss in the paranoid–schizoid experience. Projective identification brings out the ego's negative forces, and in less than optimal situations, the ego perceives the object to be overwhelmed and seeking retribution. Hope shifts to dread, and security turns into danger and loss.

This frightening feeling and phantasy is highlighted if the ego feels shut out or deprived, increasing the overall rage and subsequent envious attacks on the object. In addition, this builds a sense of spite, hate, and disappointment which pushes the ego to refuse entrance to the object. In other words, the infant feels, "If you won't give, then I refuse to take!" This projective/introjective stand-off leaves the ego in a lonely, empty, narcissistic state of loss. While feeling powerful in being able to refuse the help of the object, the ego is left to suffer feelings of abandonment and despair. If this grandiose stance is lifted, the fear becomes a phantasized punishment or retribution from the object for the ego's selfish attacks.

It is worth restating that Klein (1948, 1950) felt that the infant's primary cause of anxiety was fear of annihilation, brought on by fear of death. The self-destructive disorganization of the early ego creates a sense of impending loss of life and a terrifying disintegration. It is the consistent and reliable presence of the good object that balances this out and creates a sense of hope. The introjection and experience of the good object fortify the life instincts and the epistemophilic ego functions.

Loss and abandonment from the much-needed good object bring on both terror and rage. A primitive and pathological cycle can begin in which the infant projects its desires and unhappiness into the object. If that object is already unavailable or is now unable to process those projections, the infant feels rejected and subject to the fears of annihilation. The infant rages even more in desperation and frustration, ready to tear, eat, and swallow the object's valuable supplies. The ego phantasizes this increased hunger to have the potential to either destroy the object or cause the object to retaliate. Thus, the ego is again in a state of loss and persecution. In a vicious oral cycle, the ego feels the needed nutritive object is not only taken away leaving the ego starving, but the nutritive good object becomes spoiled food that attacks and poisons. Feelings of rage, abandonment, and betrayal flood the ego.

This type of paranoid–schizoid loss utilizes excessive splitting and PI and does not involve a true sense of guilt or remorse for hurting the object. My view is that this state of loss and attack is the essence of annihilation and compromise that Klein termed the death instinct.

Hanna Segal (1957) comments on the mental experience of the paranoid–schizoid position:

> The concept of absence hardly exists. Whenever the state of union with the ideal object is not fulfilled, what is experienced is not absence; the ego feels assailed by the counterpart of the good object—the bad object, or objects. It [the paranoid–schizoid position] is the time of the hallucinatory wish-fulfilment, described by Freud, when the thought creates objects which are then felt to be available. According to Melanie Klein, it is also the time of the bad hallucinosis when if the ideal conditions are not fulfilled, the bad object is equally hallucinated and felt as real. [p. 53]

Therefore, the loss of the union with the good object or part-objects leads to phantasies of bad objects or part-objects that attack the ego. Persecution follows loss.

Klein (1950) felt that during weaning the infant experiences loss of the first love object, the mother's breast. This is a part-object that the ego has introjected. The infant feels that he or she has destroyed the breast with greed and hatred, and this brings on depressive anxieties. In the paranoid–schizoid position, the ego is more focused on the loss of the good object and the subsequent attack of the bad object. In the depressive position, the ego is equally concerned with hurting and losing the object followed by efforts at reparation. In the paranoid–schizoid position, the ego is merely trying desperately to defend itself and survive. Reparation is beyond the scope of this type of anxiety.

Segal's (1957) comments about the ego feeling denied access to the ideal object and consequently experiencing attacking bad objects is similar to ideas proposed by Bion two years later, in 1959. He felt that the infant projected unbearable elements of fear, aggression, and confusion into the mother for containment, detoxification, and understanding. If the mother, for a variety of reasons, was unable or unwilling to act as a container for these anxieties and communications, the infantile ego was left to cope with unbearable, nameless dread. This causes fragmentation in the ego and reliance on lower level, maladaptive defences. The loss of the external container mother and the loss of the internal container mother together lead to a loss of the containment, translation, and transformation of primitive anxieties. This leaves the ego overwhelmed by intense affect, phantasies of danger and loss, and a strengthening of the death instinct. This is in contrast to the developmental benefits of maternal containment, which helps build ego structure, promotes adaptive use of PI, and creates an internalized cycle of containment and transformation between ego and object.

With the depressive position comes the integration of whole objects, awareness and worry for the other, and more complex adaptive ego abilities. When confronted with loss of the maternal object, the ego seeks substitutes (Klein, 1952c). The ego introjects the father as a whole object and a stand-in for the lost or injured mother-object. This begins a lifelong quest for alternative figures and ushers in the workings of sublimation. In this sense, the prevention of loss is the creative force behind many of humankind's endeavours. Loss instigates the life-affirming yearning for object relations, yet this occurs only if these losses are not overwhelming and if there have been enough introjected experiences of a good object to mitigate the many frustrations and losses that occur in development.

Klein (1952a) pointed out that if hatred and resentment towards the mother was the primary feeling, sublimation and substitution was difficult to obtain. Again, we see a vicious cycle. Bitterness and envy towards the mother prevent the ego from developing and attaching to other objects. At the same time, a lack of sublimation and substitution generate even more feelings of loss, envy, and rage. This produces an excessive reliance on splitting and projective identification mechanisms.

If sublimation and substitution are available to the ego, the ego is more likely met with many helpful and warm objects rather than the experience of loss. This positive internal experience enables the infant better to perceive, trust, and master the external environment. Klein (1952b) wrote: "[the infant's] repeated experiences of the external reality become the most important means of overcoming his persecutory and depressive anxieties" (p. 112). In addition, the depressive position brings with it increased awareness, concern, and love for the object. This love for the object and the new hope of restitution and restoration of the injured object mitigate the experience of internal loss (Klein, 1957). The ego is no longer felt as evil or destructive, the object appears stronger and resilient, and both ego and object are better able to withstand the vicissitudes of internal and external life.

In 1963, Klein discussed another aspect of loss associated with the mechanism of PI. Excessive use of PI, motivated by hostility or desperation, produces a fragmented ego. In bits and pieces, the ego becomes confused about what is self or object, what is bad or good, and what is internal or external. This loss of all boundaries and perception is a chronic state for the psychotic. In neurotic patients, this produces chronic loneliness and vague unease.

On the other hand, PI can be used in the service of reparation and love. As the ego enters the depressive position, concern and awareness link with whole objects. The ego is fearful of losing its precious objects through its own destructive impulses and desires. This overwhelming fear of losing the people most needed and loved in life brings out a self-restraint and a wish to preserve those objects (Klein, 1935). Creativity and altruism emerge.

In 1940, Klein wrote:

> unpleasant experiences and the lack of enjoyable ones, in the young child, especially lack of happy and close contact with loved people, increase ambivalence, diminish trust and hope and confirm anxieties about inner annihilation and external persecution; moreover they slow down and perhaps permanently check the beneficial processes through which in the long run inner security is achieved. In the process of acquiring knowledge, every new piece of experience has to be fitted into the patterns provided by the psychic reality which prevails at the time; whilst the psychic reality of the child is gradually influenced by every step in his progressive knowledge of external reality. Every such step goes along with his more and more firmly establishing his inner "good" objects, and is used by the ego as a means of overcoming the depressive position. [p. 347]

Here, Klein is emphasizing the utility of good objects in overcoming depressive anxieties. I believe that it is equally important to consider the value of good objects in helping the ego overcome paranoid–schizoid loss. Introjection and PI can create an internal environment populated by helpful and nurturing objects that help the ego traverse persecutory anxieties. On the other hand, introjection and PI can lead to an intrapsychic battlefield of predators and deadly struggles. The ego can feel capable of destroying the object and instigating a retaliation. These are phantasies of losing the object and the object's love. The ego experiences a loss of safety and attachment, brought on by the threat of attack and annihilation. Introjection of helpful and supportive objects is critical in overcoming these persecutory phantasies.

The nature of the paranoid–schizoid position means that the immature ego is dealing with part-objects and fragmented relationships. Hopefully, maturation involves a sort of collecting of good pieces of objects that give enough safety and confidence that the ego begins to integrate and move towards the experience of whole objects. Klein (1935) felt that not until the ego loves the object as a whole object can its loss be felt as a whole. However, the ego's experience with part-objects is vital to the ego's integration or disintegration. Feeling safe and fortified by multiple part-objects is crucial to proper ego development. The ego experiences the

feelings of loss with part-objects as an overwhelming bombard-
ment of multiple separations. This leads to rapid fragmentation
and internal chaos. As the good part-objects dramatically shift into
a swarm of bad part-objects, the ego's foundation is shaken apart.
Loss of the supportive background environment creates terror and
helplessness. Those objects taken for granted as helpful and necessary become a mob of persecutory traitors.

Again, paranoid–schizoid loss entails both loss of the good
part-objects and their simultaneous rebirth as deadly enemies.
Klein discussed this point in 1935 when she wrote:

> the absence of the mother arouses in the child anxiety lest it
> should be handed over to bad objects, external and internal-
> ized, either because of her death or because of her return in the
> guise of a "bad" mother. Both cases mean to the child the loss
> of the loved mother, and I would particularly draw attention
> to the fact that dread of the loss of the "good", internalized
> object becomes a source of anxiety lest the real mother should
> die. On the other hand, every experience which suggests the
> loss of the real loved object stimulates the dread of losing the
> internalized one too. [pp. 266–267]

Consistent experiences with durable, loving part-objects fortify the
ego and move it towards the depressive position, with its greater
integrative ego functions. These positive developments occur from
ongoing introjection and PI processes by which the good part-
objects and the loving feelings from the ego are brought together to
bind anxiety and strengthen the ego. Taking in and projecting love
generate maturational cycles that build psychic structure and con-
solidate trust and confidence in the internal and external world. In
favourable development, the ego's innate hostility, territoriality,
and emotional hunger are capable, through PI, of being used as
loving gifts, meaningful contact with the object, and interactive
vulnerability (Klein, 1936).

Projective identification is the strongest method of attachment
between the ego and the object. Throughout the life-span, PI allows
for important gratifying and maturational object relationships.
Through this mechanism, the ego takes part in repetitious experiences of winning and losing, taking in and letting go, feeding
and being fed, fusing and separating, approaching and avoiding,

and building up and tearing down. Safety alternates with danger, integration with disintegration.

In optimal growth, these are all in some form of balance and lead to increased ego cohesion. The depressive position is reached and worked through. For some patients, their earliest opportunities at having these complementary ties and exchanges with good objects are thwarted. This is when the potential helpers and maternal part-objects mutate into bad and withholding part-objects. As Klein has shown, this is often the result of a mixture of frustrating external environmental causes and the ego's unmanaged, excessive aggression. An unhealthy match is made through PI and is further corroded by this same mechanism. Loss becomes the background and foreground. Loss of the good part-objects leads to a sense of loss of self, and the experience of annihilation permeates the ego.

Symbolism

Symbolism and PI are intricately connected to the ego's struggles with loss. Segal (1981), in discussing the paranoid–schizoid position, writes:

> A leading defence mechanism in this phase is projective identification. In projective identification, the subject in phantasy projects large parts of himself into the object, and the object becomes identified with the parts of the self that it is felt to contain. Similarly, internal objects projected outside and identified with parts of the external world come to represent them. These first projections and identifications are the beginning of the process of symbol formation. [p. 53]

The ego uses symbol formation to deal with loss and persecutory anxiety. Symbolic functions in the ego help dilute and remove the source of pain. Sublimation, creativity, and passage into the depressive position are valuable outcomes of symbol formation. In a reciprocal manner, the more the ego uses sublimation and depressive ways of organizing experience, the more symbol formation takes place. Symbol formation within the paranoid–

schizoid position is therefore, by definition, more fragile and easily corrupted by loss and persecutory anxieties.

To make consistent and successful use of symbols, the ego must feel fortified and supported by ample good part- and whole objects. The lack of sufficient good objects strains the ego's efforts to produce symbols. If there is a significant external or internal experience of object-related trauma, the ego's functions are compromised and collapse into more primitive methods of organization. Symbol equation, in which the symbol and the object of symbolization are felt to be the same, is one such negative outcome.

Again, the ego becomes involved in a vicious cycle. Loss not only does not get worked through via symbol formation, but becomes intensified with the emergence of it. In symbolic equation (Segal, 1957), the external object is experienced as the exact same as internal objects and unconscious desires or fears. In the treatment setting, this means that there is no as-if quality to the transference, it is a psychotic transference. The ego, feeling gripped by an attacking and abandoning object that is both internal and external, is expecting loss and annihilation at every turn. Therefore, internal and external situations that contain elements of relational conflict or even potential conflict are experienced as total loss or the violent end of a crucial bond.

Patients struggling with this form of paranoid–schizoid loss, where symbol formation breaks down, will not be able to participate in humour or as-if discourse. Concrete, literal thinking has eroded and replaced this more symbolic level of communication. Metaphors such as "throwing the baby out with the bath water" evoke alarm, as the ego equates them with literally hurling a helpless baby out of a bathtub. If a session ends on a turbulent note, these patients find it difficult to imagine a temporary "truce" until analyst and patient resume the conversation next time. They feel left in a turmoil that is unresolved and continues to rage—only now they are all alone within it.

Segal (1981) writes:

> Symbol formation is an activity of the ego attempting to deal with the anxieties stirred by its relation to the object. That is primarily the fear of bad objects and the fear of the loss or inaccessibility of good objects. Disturbances in the ego's rela-

tion to objects are reflected in disturbances of symbol formation. [p. 52]

Symbol formation is a necessary ego activity to deal with object-related conflicts, including the fear of loss and attack. However, if these fears become overwhelming due to internal or external circumstances, good objects are not available and symbol formation breaks down. The more the ego fears loss and persecutory attacks, the more it needs the symbolic function. Yet, this is the very time when it collapses and the ego feels these fears becoming more and more real.

Segal (1981) writes: "In favourable circumstances of normal development, after repeated experiences of loss, recovery, and re-creation, a good object is securely established in the ego" (p. 55). Successful symbolic function helps in the recovery and re-creation of the lost object and helps to ward off persecutory phantasies. Loss of the object, grief for the lost union with that object, and the phantasies of attack and annihilation that follow all corrupt the ego's capacity to introject good objects that would build the symbolic function. This core breakdown of normal development is often precipitated by excessive use of PI based on feelings of envy and aggression as well as heavy reliance on splitting.

Segal (1981) continues to comment on normal development and symbolic function:

> This situation [of recovery and re-creation] is a powerful stimulus for the creation of symbols, and symbols acquire new functions which change their character. The symbol is needed to displace aggression from the original object, and in that way to lessen the guilt and the fear of loss. [p. 55]

Segal is pointing out the importance of symbol formation in dealing with excessive aggression towards the object. PI is the first mechanism the ego uses for this purpose. In normal development, these two mental strategies act as a reinforcement and synergist for each other. If fears of loss and persecution overwhelm the ego in the paranoid–schizoid position, PI is often used excessively and tends to erode the development of symbolic function. Without symbolic function, PI is then used more crudely and ineffectively to fight off what is felt to be real dangers and actual losses that occur over and over again.

All these relationships between symbolic function, PI, and loss are constantly in motion within the transference. In the analytic situation, the patient uses PI to deal with phantasies of loss with the analyst. Interpretation of loss and impending attack is very important in the analysis of most patients operating within the paranoid–schizoid position. The presence of symbolic function helps the treatment in that it dilutes some of the more overwhelming anxieties that occur and prevents a psychotic transference. With a breakdown of symbolic function, the transference becomes more psychotic and the patient feels that the analyst is in fact attacking and abandoning him or her.

For many patients, a successful analysis includes a working-through of paranoid fears of loss and attack and a restoration of symbolic function.

Summary

In 1936, Klein wrote:

the child mentally takes into himself—introjects—the outside world as far as he can perceive it. First he introjects the good and bad breasts, but gradually it is the whole mother . . . which he takes into himself. Along with this the father and the other people in the child's surroundings are taken in as well, to begin with in a lesser degree but in the same manner as the relation to the mother; these figures grow in importance and acquire independence in the child's mind as time goes on. If the child succeeds in establishing within himself a kind and helpful mother, this internalized mother will prove a most beneficial influence throughout his whole life. . . . I do not mean that the "internalized" good parents will consciously to be [inside], but rather as something within the personality having the nature of kindness and wisdom; this leads to confidence and trust in oneself and helps to combat and overcome the feelings of fear of having bad figures within one and of being governed by one's own uncontrollable hatred; and furthermore, this leads to trust in people in the outside world beyond the family circle. [p. 295]

These introjected good objects are constantly projected and colour how the ego perceives the world. They are then taken back in to colour the internal world. Loss of the good and helpful internal mother leaves the ego overcome by its own hatred and vulnerable to the threat of bad objects. Klein (1936) has shown that fear of the loss of the good maternal object, internal and external, is mixed with feelings of having destroyed her. The loss is therefore a punishment from the object.

My view is that this is true for the depressive position but that other anxieties regarding loss dominate the paranoid–schizoid position. In this more primitive experience, the ego feels supported by good part-objects that suddenly shift into a swarm of persecutory part-objects. This is the result of excessive hostility in the ego that the ego transports via projective identification and introjection. The union with multiple ideal objects shifts into an experience of angry, attacking objects ready to devour a helpless ego. At the moment these processes occur, the ego loses contact with the good part-objects and is left alone to fend off attacking maternal part-objects. This is the point of loss in the paranoid–schizoid position and is created by excessive PI. While PI and symbolic formation normally serve to build the ego up and fill it with enduring experiences of trust and safety, PI can also serve as the primary cause of this core ego collapse.

CHAPTER TWO

Greed, self-starvation, and the quest for safety

To illustrate my efforts at identifying and interpreting issues of loss with patients at a paranoid–schizoid level of functioning, I present here case material from my own practice. Certainly, there are multiple phantasies and transference themes happening at any given clinical moment. However, I demonstrate the patient's unconscious struggle with primitive feelings of loss.

The threat of internal loss—death of the self and the object—fuels drastic and desperate psychological measures. The paranoid–schizoid ego feels capable of destroying the object with its oral rage, greed, and desire. This is a phantasy of one's tremendous hunger for love, nourishment, and power being met with revenge and retaliation. It is a phantasy of betrayal, loss, and persecution that ultimately leads to an experience of annihilation. Excessive projective identification is a common coping mechanism. Splitting, denial, and projection of oral greed and demand for idealism protects the object temporarily. This translates to a masochistic request for tolerance and forgiveness from the object. However, the ego quickly feels even more persecuted. As the ego's level of rage, greed, and hunger escalate, more projection and splitting is needed, creating a more ominous and demanding object. Anxiety over loss, conflict, and catastrophe feeds on itself.

"Miss R"

The patient, Miss R, is in twice-a-week psychoanalytic psycho-therapy. She experiences intense paranoid–schizoid conflicts and relates to me in masochistic and hysterical ways. She often feels depressed and is prone to panic attacks, suicidal thoughts, and acting out. In the transference, she feels safe, understood, and warm, only to later feel bullied, afraid, and distant. In other words, internally there is a sudden shift from security to betrayal.

Miss R takes medication for anxiety and depression. She some-times thinks that the medication helps her a great deal, and other times hates being on it and wants to stop. She thinks I disapprove of it.

Miss R related a dream at the beginning of a recent session. As with all dreams, the context and nature of the transference is im-portant to consider. Last week, she came in for an extra session because she felt despondent over her job and her relationship to her brother. She told me that the extra time helped and that being with me made her feel safe and calm. This week, she came in saying she didn't want to be in treatment and almost didn't come to the session. After protesting about having to be in therapy and saying she didn't trust me, she presented a dream:

> I have to take some type of medication. I don't want to but I have to. I want to not take it, but I have to. It starts rotting out all my teeth. They get thin and develop holes in them that get bigger and bigger. Most of my teeth start falling out of my head, just rotted away. Not all of them, but most of them. It's horrible, they just rot and fall out. But, I don't tell anyone. I keep it to myself. I don't want anyone to know.

She then fell silent. Eventually, she said, "It's a weird dream and probably has to do with my medication." She then went on to another subject.

During my countertransference/reverie, I had three different associations to her dream:

1. Her father doing something sexual to her when she was a young girl, perhaps oral sex. She keeps it a secret. (There is a history of emotional and sexual abuse, but I think I was picking up on her own oral urges as well.)

2. Losing her teeth symbolizes a loss of power, aggression, and autonomy. She submits to the will of another, and her oral desires are taken away. Yet she keeps it all a secret, as though the secret is her way of remaining in power.

3. I think I am doing something to her that she likes, but then dislikes. She turns her positive transference and active sexual feelings for me into something bad and passive, something she is a victim of. Through PI, she puts her sexual and aggressive feelings into me and then feels attacked and victimized. She wants to defend herself and fight back, but she is scared that she will hurt me. Therefore, she not only puts her teeth into me and feels I am after her, but she feels it is bad and dangerous to have teeth, and so she destroys them. Keeping it all a secret is a way to play a behind-the-scenes sadomasochistic game with me.

I give her the third association

She said she agrees with my ideas, and she elaborated on them a bit. Then she said its also about her lose of confidence and fear of being more assertive (Association 2). Finally, she said she thinks the dream might be something about her father and about something sexual and dirty (Association 3).

I commented on how her desires to be with me and have us together gets reversed into something bad and scary—suddenly, I want something from her. I said that this may mean she has strong needs and wishes that she puts into me and then feels hunted down by them and gets scared of me. She agreed and elaborated a bit more until the session was over.

The next session, she reported how she thought of me in a loving and friendly way during the week, but now that she was with me she feared I would do bad things to her, make her upset, or force her to look at her past. She also told me about her new rental agreement, which she had to assertively ask her landlord for. I commented that she had got her teeth back. She agreed and told me two new dreams. In the first one,

> I keep telling her that her fear about her boyfriend cheating on her is unfounded and she just needs to trust people and ignore her irrational fears that are "all in her head". As I repeat this to her, she keeps hearing the voices of her boyfriend and another woman in the bedroom. I tell her to ignore this as it is just her lack of trust in people. She hears the voices again. I tell her she is being silly. She finally opens the bedroom door and finds her boyfriend with another woman.

She told me that the dream shows how I have forced her to ignore her own intuition. I said that the dream also shows her being betrayed and that I tricked her. I commented that there are different sides to the dream. It is also her in the bed, but she doesn't like to face her own desires and instead turns it into a passive victimization. She agreed and said that, while she knows that is true, it makes her feel like a pervert and she feels really awful and wants to get rid of all those thoughts.

I commented that while many of our recent sessions have been about me championing reality and her fighting to deny it, in the dream she reverses those roles and I champion denial and she fights for the truth. However, she blames me for what I do in reality and in her dream. Again, she is the victim with no ownership. I tell her that she may fear an even greater loss and trauma if she were to feel assertive or active with me.

After discussing this new dream for a while, she told me the second new dream.

> We are at my house and being very warm and friendly. I am showing her my art collection and it all feels very nice and close. Then, it suddenly becomes sexual. I make advances and she feels panicked and shocked.

The dream ends. She falls silent. I commented on how she puts (through PI) her desires into me and fears that I am a pervert, when she may be having those feelings about me but is shocked and scared of them. She said this is true but she is so repulsed and

disgusted at herself that she wants to change the subject. I commented that our plans to start working together more frequently
may be part of what is fuelling her dreams. She is both excited and
fearful of our plans. She has phantasies about what we will do and
how close we may get, but she is scared that her urges and feelings
may get out of hand and spoil our relationship. She fears there
could be a break in the safe bond, a loss, and a sudden trauma in
its place.

I later thought of how this second dream is a semi-reparation
and defence against the first dream. It also simply repeats the same
themes of trust and betrayal, lust and denial, power and boundaries. Finally, by being silent and having me make the first interpretative "move", she gets me to be the seducer and she the passive
victim of my actions.

The predominate theme of these dreams centres around her
phantasy of the lost ideal object. She wishes for me to be all loving
and trustworthy, but this intimacy is lost and replaced by a mean
and dishonest analyst. These fears appear to be the result of a
history of external trauma and betrayal mixing with the projection
of strong oral aggression and sexual wishes put into me. She envi-
sions me as overwhelmed by these demands and transformed into
an angry and lustful person.

This patient's phantasies, fears, and desires are managed by her
ego's reliance on PI. She tries to shift responsibility, blame, and
motivation to the object by projecting out her active phantasies.
She then feels threatened by what she thought was a protecting
ideal object. Therefore, she activates an inner experience of loss by
her use of PI. Due to splitting mechanisms, she creates an ideal
object that is then torn down by her aggression, rage, envy, and
sexual desires. At this point in treatment, she is able to take in my
interpretations enough to neutralize some of these internal trau-
mas. However, her destructive use of PI and her lack of adequate
internal good objects create a drain on my ability to act as a sufficient mental container for her projections.

Many paranoid–schizoid patients, such as this case of Miss R,
are caught in a cycle of desire, dread, loss, and persecution. Projective identification offers them a temporary respite from fears of
total loss and inner collapse. However, the trade-off is a self-starv-
ing, a denial of need or hunger. Miss R had to frantically deny and

project her excitement over sexual desire, wishes for emotional union, and interpersonal conquest. This resulted in her feeling victimized and at the mercy of all the objects she had idealized. She tried to control, own, and eat up those objects, and, through excessive, pathological cycles of splitting and projection, they had come to control, own, and devour her.

Her oral drives created anxieties over the loss of the good internal relationship and terror over the bad enemy that replaced it. Miss R experienced her own search for autonomy as an invitation for trouble, rejection, and self-destruction. This phantasy clouded the transference as well, where she felt that insight and growth were potentially dangerous. By erasing all evidence of personal worth, creativity, and interest, she felt temporarily safe from me becoming an unpredictable, hurtful, and possibly deadly object.

CHAPTER THREE

Idealization, devaluation, and the narcissistic stance

Some patients are always on the alert, fearful that their objects are about to betray them, reject them, and hurt them. They want to trust their objects and look up to them, but they cannot get past the tremendous anxiety that what is good will become bad and what is stable will shatter. Again, this phantasy has dual elements that feed off each other. Loss of the trusted, idealized object is felt as a critical rejection and abandonment. Due to the subsequent projection of rage, greed, and envy, the object then becomes transformed into a venomous monster, returning for revenge.

The following case involves a patient, "Tony", who took a "just-in-case" approach to life. He was, unconsciously, so anxious about these transformations of supportive objects into bad ones that he always tried to prevent it ahead of time. This led to constant preventative strategies and ways of offering atonement to others when it really was not needed. He truly believed that relationships would always sour at some point, so he was more interested in looking for evidence of the souring than of relationships building.

In the transference, Tony tried hard to appease me, especially in the early stages of treatment. Another strategy he used was to deny any emotional attachment to me, claiming it was "only therapy". By unlinking us emotionally, he could magically prevent any forthcoming loss of me as a good object and stop me from turning against him.

Another phantasy that these types of patients often struggle with is the idea that individuation will increase their risk of being abandoned and hurt. Therefore, Tony tried in many various ways to deny our separate identities. He tried to make us one in his mind to avoid the danger that our separation could bring. This made it difficult for us to have different ideas or opinions and crippled our ability to negotiate and be creative. For patients like Tony, they unconsciously believe that this is a small price to pay to reduce the risk of the destructive loss they imagine is so close.

"Tony"

Tony was 40 years old when he decided to see me for help with his depression. He had felt hopeless for many years and was now unsure if he could manage his stressful bank job. He alternated between wanting to quit his job and kill himself, or hoping one day to become the vice-president. I treated him analytically, three times a week, for five years. He suffered from chronic constipation and asthma and was subject to paranoid outbursts. Tony told me that his mother had always boasted of being able to read minds and tell the future. He felt that he had similar powers.

Tony was the oldest of four children and was raised by his mother. Tony's father had a sales job that took him out of town for days or weeks at a time. He was a self-centred and sadistic alcoholic. No matter what Tony did, whether he tried at sports, academics, or social activities, his father found fault. It seemed that his father resented anyone who had an identity of their own. He saw people as weak and pathetic. Tony's mother was quiet and kept to herself, helping the children out and trying to keep out of her husband's way. Tony remembered being angry and wanting to always run away from home to "get away from those losers".

The first years of treatment with Tony were difficult. He segmented life into countless emergencies that he insisted were never related to each other. Everything seemed to go wrong with his life. Work, dating, and day-to-day life all took on an "if it can collapse, it will" quality. Tony felt that I could easily be upset with him, so he tried hard to be a good, dutiful patient. He looked like someone who was on his way to the principal's office. He would quickly apologize for imagined mistakes ahead of time, as a preventative. If there was a problem somewhere, he seized the opportunity to blame himself and then beg forgiveness. When a neighbour's dog was run over, he cried that it might as well be his fault. He felt that he could have saved it had he been in the area on that day, at that time.

When I interpreted some of his feelings as a cover-up for potentially hostile or destructive urges, he insisted that I was "way off base". When I wondered about how he managed to take responsibility for any and all grief in his vicinity, he told me he didn't know what I meant. Even when he began to show open disgust and hostility towards his mother and younger sister for how "weak and stupid" they were, he dismissed his feelings as being normal.

At first, I was kept as a authority figure to be respected and treated with caution. Tony insisted that I was his doctor and he had no other feelings for me. After the second year, Tony began to show more willingness to talk about his phantasies and his feelings towards me. In addition, he started to be condescending and angry with me. If I drew his attention to it, he denied it. He would tell me that he was just having a bad day or that any normal person would feel the same way.

Tony felt disdain for others and the things they enjoyed. For example, he would complain about how ridiculous the old television show *I Love Lucy* was. Tony said, "It is ludicrous to have a show about a group of misfits who did nothing but waste their lives. They never do anything productive, they are a bunch of losers. What right do they have to take up valuable TV time!" The humorous characters were taken seriously and then ridiculed. I was asked to be his audience, as he fussed and fumed over these intolerable insults to his outlook on proper living.

In a similar way, Tony would tell me, with fury, about how deficient he was at the bank. He was sure he was the worst bank officer they had ever had. When I commented on the rage he was feeling, he turned it on me and yelled, "I am not angry, what the hell makes you think that?"

Over the next few years, Tony alternated between judging himself, judging me, or judging others. Usually, he did all three. My interpretations were felt to be pathetic nonsense, attacking jabs, or something totally impossible to understand. Gradually and sporadically, he did begin using some of my comments. When I pointed out that he switched back and forth between being his angry, judgemental father and being a frightened, self-punitive, little boy, he seemed unable to take it in. He ignored me. However, as time went on, he started to use my comments as his own. Tony would claim to have a new insight—one that I had brought up previously. Eventually, we understood that if he accepted my comments he felt mentally invaded. My interpretations had to be under his control before he could allow them to exist. This was a protective manoeuvre to avoid any dependency or vulnerability. He was convinced that a peaceful or gratifying dependence would turn into something dangerous.

This more paranoid fear would escalate if I asked too many questions. He would yell at me, "You are always forcing me to reconsider my thoughts, why can't you leave my mind alone?" He would feel interrogated and shout, "Why aren't my answers good enough for you? Why doesn't everyone just leave me alone?" Each word I used could have hidden meaning and negative implications. On rare occasions, he would feel thankful to see me and tell me how much of an oasis I provided against the harsh world. Most hours, I was a cruel person who never helped him, and it would only be a matter of time before he quit. He would then settle the matter by saying, "I guess I will just have to endure your shit till the bitter end, when you finally let me go."

Tony's attacks on me paralleled his attacks on himself. He would tell me what a lazy, fat slob he was. He felt the only solution was to push and force himself to work as hard as possible seven days a week to prove to himself and those around him that he could be a decent human being.

When arriving for his session, Tony often has harrowing tales of how he barely avoided a "bloody catastrophe" of car wrecks and fights for parking spaces. When I comment on his feeling oppressed, panicked, or worried, Tony usually dismisses my idea by saying, "I have no idea what your talking about, I don't feel like that at all."

At other times, Tony has been able to respond to both here-and-now interpretations as well as genetic reconstructions. I told him that he must see the world as a constant threat and worry about losing my acceptance, and therefore he tries to make up and apologize just in case. Tony agreed. I mentioned that he may be recreating his relationship with his father in our meetings. He said, "The worst thing about my father was the constant possibility of a crisis." He went on to tell me about how tension and blame was always "looming" around the corner. Again, he feared that his idealized object would easily and predictably shift into an attacking and judging bad object.

As the years passed, Tony was more able to think about his feelings. He felt less lost in his terrifying and angry phantasies. He told me of how he magically connects separate events throughout the day to create a way to confirm his view of himself as cursed and bad. He didn't say hello to a co-worker one morning, and that person suffered a skiing accident over the weekend. Tony was convinced that he was involved, by way of neglect. This illustrates how Tony mostly lived with the phantasy of loss and his own destructive capacities. Tragedy and warfare were always around the corner. For Tony, this also hid his loneliness and his longings for a predictable and peaceful object he could join with. He tried to beat the bad object to the punch, by always imagining himself as bad and worthless. This prevented him from experiencing the jolting loss of his wished-for ideal object.

A typical session

P: I am really sorry I didn't make it last time. My stupid co-workers at the bank walked out on me and left me with everything. I was stuck at work. I was really angry that I couldn't make it and that I let you down, especially after I promised to never be late again. It just seems that things don't ever go right for me. I really tried hard. I told them in advance that I had to leave.

A: You seem to want me to know how hard you tried, since you feel you really let me down.

P: Well, I am really angry at my co-workers for just doing whatever they please and leaving me there to pick up the pieces. I seem to be the one that always gets stuck with everything. Somebody has to be responsible, but why does it always have to be me? I really do want to be here and then I couldn't make it. It spoiled my whole week. I was furious.

A: You are more aware of your anger when you feel violated. [*Normally, he would deny any negative feelings.*]

P: I don't want to go around yelling at everyone, even though I was livid. I have been filling in for all the people who are on vacation. I don't ask for much, but I never get my turn.

A: You imagine your feelings would explode if you were to express them.

P: Well, I guess its hard to imagine talking to my co-workers about this without just screaming at them. It's just that they don't seem to care. Sure, I would like to just walk out sometimes, but I try and care and be responsible.

A: You want me to know that you really care about your treatment and your commitment to our work together.

P: Well, yes. I want you to realize that. My father never seemed to give a shit about anything. He would never follow through. I never asked for much really, but he didn't seem to really care unless it was about him or something he wanted. He was always drunk and in a foul mood.

A: You are afraid that I see you that way, as irresponsible and not giving a damn.

P: Yes. I guess I worry that you see me like my father was. In the beginning I felt like you might be like my father, but I have gotten over that. You don't give me any evidence to think that way, but I am worried that you see me like my father was.

A: Maybe that fear keeps you from being able to negotiate with your peers at work.

P: Well, yes. I have this weird illogical fear that if I express my anger at them I will be punished in a way that will be much worse than the way it was to begin with, so I figure the best thing to do is just grin and bear it. [*The thin connection to the object can easily be broken, bringing on internal calamity.*]

In the last session I had made the recommendation that he come in more often, and he said he didn't know "how to take that".

A: I notice you haven't brought up your concerns about coming in more often.

P: Oh. Well, I didn't really want to think about it. It felt kind of weird, strange, or ominous. I didn't really understand why you suggested that, and so I think that I tried to secretly guess what you meant.

A: What were your guesses?

P: Oh, I didn't really come up with much. It just felt weird. I started to feel really strange and tense.

A: You are wondering or worried about the nature of our relationship?

P: No, it's just that when you said that it made me realize, this is therapy. I am not just here hanging out with a friend or dating a girlfriend. It was kind of a jolt, a shock. It's just business. [*He seems worried that our connection is gone and was just a sham.*]

A: Maybe you have been feeling some trust and security and now you worry if that is real.

P: Well, I have started to kind of relax and trust this . It just felt so weird. It's hard to describe. I thought you might have some kind of agenda or plan. [*Here, he seems anxious about a potential threat or betrayal of some kind.*]

A: Such as?

P: I don't know. When things are unpredictable I don't like it. I feel like it comes out of the blue.

A: So our relationship had become a bit predictable, even safe. Then you suddenly felt like your sense of security and trust crumbled.

P: Yeah. It's just so strange. It was such a surprise.

Tony began to imagine that our relationship had changed to something he should approach with caution. He felt I might have betrayed him. When I suggested we meet more often, the increased intimacy meant a potential break in the safety or trust between us.

A year later

During a session about a year later, Tony revealed his intense identification with the grandiosity and rage of the combined maternal/paternal object. He looked down on me and felt that I was worthless. At the same time, it was evident that he did so out of enormous anxiety and the sense that I could easily invade and monopolize his mind.

In this session I made an interpretation that, on reflection, was an insult to Tony's view of himself. He felt that he was untouchable and above the influence of others. This protected him from his core sense of being attacked, manipulated, and abandoned by his objects. In my technical error, which was no doubt brought on by a PI process, I essentially told him that he was weak and unaware of the dangers around him. This, of course, made him extremely anxious and confirmed his phantasies about being vulnerable to attack and abandonment.

P: My boss is so easygoing, slow-moving, patient, and really nice. I wonder what it would be like to have him as a father. If I made a mistake as his son, he probably would say, "Oh, don't worry about it, it's ok." He would be gentle. He is so calm and easygoing that I don't know how to relate to him. It feels so odd.

A: Do you think that given what a chaotic childhood you had, being with someone who is so easygoing feels confusing? [*Here, I make the mistake of questioning his omnipotence.*]

Tony exploded and spent the rest of the hour yelling at me for being so "stupid, judgemental, and ignorant".

P: I am tired of you putting me through this type of stupid, fucking mind game. You keep trying to make me rethink things that I have already decided on. You keep trying to force me to rethink things that I have settled on and don't think twice about. What right do you have!

A: Perhaps I am bringing up feelings that are unacceptable to you.

P: If I had thought of these ideas before, and I didn't, I already would have decided they didn't belong there anyway. Now you are judging me for that and trying to change my mind. You want me to think that I am the prisoner on my mind, where I am stripped of any and all self-agency. How dare you! [*After a long silence, he mentions a comment his boss made at work.*] He said I can be a little hyperactive at times. I am now focusing on that with a vengeance!

A: Just as you are feeling vengeful about the remarks I made today.

P: Basically, if you or anyone else on this fucking planet doesn't think exactly like I do, I am outraged. I am right, so I don't want to hear differently.

A: If we aren't one, that disturbs you.

P: Yes, that is right.

Tony attempted to maintain a narcissistic, symbiotic state with all his objects. This erased any differences between him and his objects and gave him a feeling of safety and power. Without this, he experienced a threatening differentiation that he viewed as a loss of safety. If there was a difference between people, there could also be disputes, anger, and abandonment. Therefore, Tony tried his best to keep his objects under his control and identical to him in thought and feeling. It is a world of blissful unity or dangerous difference.

Without his delusional, narcissistic state, he had to face the fall of his idealized internal object and the rise of vicious, persecutory objects. He was so envious and judgemental that when he projected these feelings into his objects, he felt surrounded by traitors and thugs. These phantasies combined with his history of family abuse and trauma to make for a very precarious relationship to his internal and external objects.

CHAPTER FOUR

Vulnerability, union,
and the return of the bad object

In optimal development, a child is brought up in a family that respects the child's needs and natural vulnerabilities. Even if the parents do not fully understand the child's oral striving and the inherent mix of hostility, love, greed, and giving that children exhibit, they can respect these feelings. Acknowledgement, respect, and curiosity on the care-givers' part leave a sense of being wanted and feeling safe and fulfilled in the child's developing ego. This positive cycle can be seen with adult patients in the transference. If the analyst respects the patient's day-to-day display of envy, despair, altruism, desire, competition, and so forth, and appreciates it all with curiosity, the patient usually feels cared for and is able to continue exploring him/herself in a vulnerable and honest manner.

The paranoid–schizoid patients I am describing have not been so fortunate in their childhood histories. Consequently, their transference experiences tend to be much more guarded, rocky, and mistrusting. The next case example, "Mr E", shows how one such patient grappled with his phantasies of loss, judgement, and attack. In the early stages of treatment, he tried to protect himself from these dangers by being super self-sufficient and independent.

If he did not need me, I could not hurt him. Instead of the partial loss/atonement and restoration of object/healing of relationship that is typical of depressive-position phantasies, Mr E warded off phantasies of an ideal, yet fragile object that splintered and broke down in a permanent way. This left him lost, forsaken, and in danger. In this empty state, he felt he was then at the mercy of judgmental and angry objects working to control and destroy him.

Bit by bit, with hard work on both our parts, Mr E was able to feel less anxious and more able to drop his manic defence. This enabled him to look more seriously at our relationship and the intrapsychic meaning it had for him. His second dream illustrates a moment in which he was able to drop the manic defence. However, his basic paranoid–schizoid phantasy of loss remained and resurfaced when he became more vulnerable. In the dream, at first he is able to enjoy a new closeness to me, but then he feels a renewed criticism and attack. I change from an inviting, warm object to a cold and cruel one. This is the essence of the paranoid–schizoid experience of loss. It is the abandonment of love and its replacement with persecutory scorn and hate.

"Mr E"

Mr E is a obsessive man in his early thirties, given to paranoia and severe control issues. He entered treatment for help with his failed relationships. He has been in twice-a-week psychoanalytic psychotherapy for two years.

Mr E is constantly battling his internal objects for power and dominance. He projects his angry, demanding, and competitive feelings into the object, creating a world of selfish opportunists. Therefore, he is frightened of becoming close to anyone for fear of giving up his power, being attacked, or having someone become clingy. He is somewhat concerned about hurting his objects, but it is mostly a way of trying to prove how caring and honest he is. In other words, he used depressive ways of relating as a smokescreen for his more sadistic paranoid–schizoid methods of operating.

Mr E's transference and his general approach to life is rigidly focused on always trying to defend himself against the potential

loss of his idealized objects. By never trusting anyone and by hurting others first, he feels he can prevent the change of a hoped-for
ideal object into a persecutory one.

In the transference, he tries never to show any neediness or
dependence on me. He tries to be self-contained and omnipotent.
Rather than needing my help, he thinks of himself as using me to
achieve a better persona. Over the years, he plays various power
games with me, such as always coming five minutes late to show
that he is in charge and will not "submit" to waiting in the waiting-
room. By being late, he makes me wait instead. Again, he won't
allow me to become an object that he needs and depends on, as he
feels that that would open him up to the threat of tremendous loss,
betrayal, and attack. Naturally, all his intimate relationships fail
because he refuses to give, be vulnerable, or compromise on issues.
The most current external context in which his material can be
understood is that he broke up with another girlfriend due to these
same problems. In an internal context, he has been much more able
to show me through words, rather than action, his fear of being
taken over, his anal sadism, and his hope for acceptance and love.

Recently, he presented the following dream:

> I was in the kitchen and this guy tells me, "I will show you how to
> cook a bird." So I am just standing there while this guy takes a live
> bird and puts it on a big dish and surrounds it with fruit salad. Then
> he puts the dish into the oven at 350 degrees. As the oven heats up, the
> bird starts to get really hot and burning. So, bit by bit, the bird starts
> to eat the fruit salad to stay cool and hydrated. Eventually, the bird
> runs out of fruit and dies from the heat. Then the guy pulls the dish
> out of the oven and says, "See, now you have oven-cooked bird, stuffed
> with fruit." That was the end of the dream.

Mr E said it was "a really weird dream", and he had no idea what
it was about.

Over the course of the session, I made the following interpretation of the PI transference process that was acted out within the
dream. I commented on how the dream represents his relationship
to himself and to me. If the bird was an ordinary bird, it would
have begun screaming and flapping its wings and trying very hard
to get out of the oven. In this way, it would be crying for help and

would certainly need somebody to open the oven door. But this bird is like Mr. E. It refuses to admit to being in pain and tries to be totally self-sufficient by eating the fruit. It is as if the bird is saying, "I don't need you and the heat is certainly no bother. I will just sit here and eat my fruit. I am above it all."

I also commented that the dream is about the treatment in that he feels trapped and cooked in his own juices with me if he exposes his true self. He acts self-sufficient and grandiose with me and seems to have no use for me. I told him that he is also the sadistic cook and the victimized bird at the same time. This may relate to his feelings about his sadistic father and how victimized he felt as a child. Next, I told him I was the helpless listener, who has to watch and listen to him, the cruel cook. Finally, I told him he tries to best others and be above others and never need anyone, but this always leaves him feeling like the stuffed bird, "full of false pride and dead from a hollow victory".

It was the end of the session. He agreed with what I had said. He replied, "It is all true, but I don't want to risk trying it differently." In my countertransference, I felt as I imagine he does most of the time: hopeless, powerless, and stuck, like a cooked goose.

Ironically, I had to cancel our next session due to food poisoning. He left me a message saying he was sorry, unconsciously viewing himself as the chef who poisoned me. During his message, he told me that things had become much worse because he and his girlfriend had had a big fight. He said he was eager to talk to me about it.

When we met, he told me he was surprised to have had a dream with me in it:

He dreamed of suddenly being taken along by a group of friends for a ride in the car. He didn't know why he was going or where he was going. He felt confused about the purpose of the trip and was literally "just along for the ride". Eventually, the car came to a house and the friends informed him that they were all there to visit somebody. They knocked on the door and I came out. My patient suddenly realized he had wound up at my house. Mr E felt frightened because he "knew he wasn't supposed to know anything about me" but now he had violated that rule. I came out of my house and shook everyone's hands. When I came to him, I glared at him in a hateful, angry way.

Mr E said he was so surprised to have a dream with me in it, and he thought it might be brought on by the fact that we didn't meet. When I asked him for more associations, he said he couldn't think of anything but that my glaring, angry eyes were scary.

I told Mr E the following. He was scared that he could hurt me if he was too dependent or too demanding. That, in some way, he may have felt responsible for my poisoning. In the dream, he was the passive passenger without any motive or destination. He put his motives into his friends, and they were active. This was to disguise his own active wish to see me, to know more about me, and to have me help him. This wish scared him because he thought I would be angry and punish him if I realized how much he did want to have a connection.

Mr E told me that this was probably true, because he would be angry if anyone got too needy with him, as they would feel like "a leech". He then went on to tell me about his fight with his girl-friend and how he worried he had hurt her as well. He alternated between feeling bad that he had been cold and mean to her and then to feeling angry at her and that she deserved to be punished for being such a "leech".

So, once again, Mr E's ideal object is fragile and easily turns from a hoped-for helper to a angry punisher. It seems that his oral and anal desires feel overwhelming and threaten the object, de-stroying the love or compassion and engendering hate and revenge. This is split off from the part of him that treats needy, helpless objects with disdain and sadism. These two separated aspects of his ego oscillate rapidly, creating a difficult sadomaso-chistic transference. This is continuously reconfigured by PI and the threat of both loss and persecution.

CHAPTER FIVE

Love, hate, and the dread
of impending annihilation

Three short case reports are used in this chapter to show ways that paranoid–schizoid patients fight off the supportive presence of the analyst in order to avoid persecutory experiences of loss. This makes for difficult countertransference issues, chronic resistance to treatment, and premature termination and aborted treatments. These patients suffer a great deal. They dread being misunderstood, as this equates to being abandoned and betrayed. This fear of a nameless dread leads to subtle or not so subtle demands for agreement at all costs. This leads to an air of domination and submission in the treatment process. These patients cannot tolerate separateness, and they desire an idealistic state of agreement between ego and object. Envy and excessive projective identification play a large part of the dysfunctional interactions with the analyst and other major figures in their lives. Thinking is necessary for a working-through process. However, for these patients, thinking is anxiety provoking as it brings them into awareness of the differences between self and object. This triggers the phantasies of loss and attack. All this promotes a jerky and hard-to-contain pattern of "I want you—stay away and leave me alone" kind of transference.

"Wallis"

Wallis had been in analysis for several years before telling me the dream discussed below. She often yearned for a "perfect emotional feed" with her analyst. This intense oral desire was matched by an equally intense fear of the analyst suddenly turning into a persecuting stranger. This was partly based on her fears of destroying the object by being too needy and partly on the introjection of a mother who could easily become angry and rejecting.

On and off for months, Wallis had told her analyst of plans to "take a break" from treatment or to cut back on the number of sessions. She felt overwhelmed by the analysis and felt forced to attend. At other times, she felt she could easily come seven days a week for the rest of her life.

Wallis presented a dream *of coming to her appointment and having her analyst announce he was about to try a new technique. This involved stopping treatment altogether for twelve weeks. At that time they would resume and explore the consequences. The analyst seemed oblivious to any possible effect this announcement or the new technique might have on Wallis.*

Wallis felt devastated. In the dream, she felt *"cast out into the cold sea, dying alone in the darkness"*. She reached over to a plant in the analyst's office. She broke the plant in two and huddled with her portion. She kept it as a remnant of him and as revenge for being rejected.

Analysis of the dream showed that she had projected her angry and rejecting parts into the analyst and felt cast aside by him. This sudden loss was shattering. While Wallis tried to fight back by hurting the analyst's property, she mainly clung to whatever remnants of the analyst she could find. The loss of the good object was sudden and was experienced as a purposeful abandonment. She felt he had been replaced with a bad and punishing object.

"Ruby"

Ruby grew up in a poor family with five brothers and four sisters. Her father was an angry man whom she remembers as always picking on her and putting her down. Ruby longed for his love and approval but was scared of his critical and often violent ways. Her mother would appear to be attentive and caring, but would then switch to being hostile and judgemental. Ruby remembers her mother sexually stimulating her in the bathroom, under the premise of good hygiene. To this day, Ruby maintains an extremely stormy relationship with her mother. Ruby tries to get close and then feel rejected. Things easily turn from sweet to sour.

I saw Ruby in psychoanalytic treatment for seven years. She broke off the treatment several times when she became psychotic and paranoid. If she was early for her appointment and I hadn't yet arrived, she felt that this meant I had rejected her. She would then yell at me for being late. In other words, if I wasn't present when she arrived, I was bad. She wanted me on command. This demanding way of relating also served to protect herself from the risk of losing me. Ruby told me that she "knew" I hated her and just wanted to get rid of her. Other times, she felt grateful that I was willing to see her and felt a special fondness for me. This masochistic trust easily crumbled, and I became a rejecting judge.

Ruby's acting out dominated the treatment. She binged on sweets and cakes until she weighed close to a hundred and forty kilos. This and other somatic enclaves shaped our time together, protecting her from the overwhelming anxieties she lived with. It was safer to talk about diets than about her fear of our relationship.

Ruby was so afraid of being abandoned and attacked by her objects that she made sure to escape before it happened. She would sabotage her performance at work, so she was fired from almost every job she managed to get. Unconsciously, she also managed to beat people to the punch in that she would ruin her relationships and leave her friends before they could leave her. Ruby was able to orchestrate an endless series of crisis and disaster in her daily living, all of which made it impossible for her to be attached to her objects for any length of time.

Ruby managed to repeat this in the transference. I tried to show her how, through projective identification, she would project the hurt, mistreated, and abandoned little girl part of herself into her analyst and begin to bully and blame her analyst like a mean parent would. Other times, she would project the volatile, rejecting parent part of herself into the analyst and feel threatened and hurt. Her psychosis, depression, eating disorder, assorted delusions, and conversion symptoms all stemmed from her core phantasy that she would find herself with a good loving object that would suddenly change into a cold, rejecting, and attacking object. Ruby summed this up when she told me, "We will eventually have to end this therapy. One day it will be over and I will be left all alone. What feels so good will one day turn to shit and I will be all alone. So why the hell should I invest myself into it in the first place?"

This intrapsychic paradigm of loss shaped her daily experiences. She felt that a lucky glimpse of a friendly, loving object was sure to be eclipsed by an angry and rejecting object.

"Sidney"

Sidney came to treatment in his early thirties, wanting help with his sense of "being stuck in life". He was unable to move ahead in his career and had never been in a satisfying relationship.

Sidney was the younger of two brothers, and his father was a moody, dominating, alcoholic who "ran a tight ship". This meant that father ordered the family around and beat anyone who questioned his authority. Sidney had learned to be quiet and follow his father's orders, watching his rebellious brother be beaten for speaking out. Sidney's mother was a fragile woman who had given up her career hopes to be married. She followed her husband's orders and tried to keep the family peace.

Sidney felt that his mother was unable to function in life and needed him to be her emotional mast and rudder. Sidney felt he sacrificed his life to save hers. He told me, "Mother shaped me into the little man she wanted her husband to be. I became her rock that she could depend on. I had to give up my identity to make sure she was happy." My impression was that Sidney couldn't use his mother or his father as an idealized object and in fact grew to despise both of them. However, unconsciously he was scared that if he discarded them, his mother would die and his father would retaliate. He felt he had a great power that could affect others' lives. Therefore, he became an expert at pretending to respect others while secretly defacing them.

As the treatment continued, Sidney was plainly rageful and scared. He only dated women he knew he could manipulate and reject. He felt powerful when abusing them, but ended up empty and envious of others who had fulfilling relationships. In his job, he felt that he was the one who held the company up. Without his hard work and sacrifice, they would probably go under. In other words, at work he repeated his masochistic mother–son relationship. In dating, he not only identified with his angry father but also took revenge on his mother by tormenting and controlling women. This desire for revenge extended to elaborate phantasies of beating and torturing anyone who frustrated him.

To strangers, he felt driven to go the extra mile to help out or be generous. He was the perfect boy scout. But, with those he became close to, including his analyst, he was shrewd, manipulative, and sadistic. Through PI, he also felt that he was uniquely special and wonderfully honest while the rest of the world was dangerous, dishonest, and pedestrian.

Throughout the first year, Sidney was irritated and arrogant when I made references to our relationship. He told me that I was simply there to do my job. I felt he meant, "Shut up and fix me, that is what I pay you for." In the second year of his analysis, it became clear that he used PI as a defence against loss. He projected the intimidated and lonely little-boy parts of himself into me and identified with the dominating, cold aspects of his father. In this way, he owned me and ordered me around to fix his psyche. This was all in the service of protecting him from becoming dependent on me and facing the dangers that came with that. He began to tell me how scared he was that I would seize the opportunity to control him. He felt he would lose his identity if he were to "let down his shield" with me.

I interpreted these phantasies by showing him how behind his defence of an angry father/bullied little-boy bond was a fear of being taken over by a greedy mother. He placed his own oral neediness and aggression along with his image of a clinging, needy mother into me. This left him with his original childhood feeling of losing his sense of self and becoming absorbed by mother. This loss of the good maternal object that was truly invested in him as an individual (a loss of love and interest) combined with his own fear of destroying his fragile mother with his own deep oral hunger (a loss of the object and consequently of the self). Therefore, he dreaded the moment of loss in which the good object vanished and the bad object appeared.

After several years he said, "I know I have many feelings. But I hide them with hate, anger, control, and distance. What if I actually share my feelings with you and you go away. Or I go away. I would be hurt, I would suffer. If something changes, I could be really hurt. If I hurt you and you decide you've had enough . . . I want you to be here with me, but what if you get overwhelmed by it all and choose to leave . . . or are hurt permanently?" This was a real shift in trust. He revealed how scared he was. What he wished for so much could be taken away and replaced by pain. He wasn't sure who would hurt whom and how revenge might happen, but it all seemed like too big of a risk. To hope for me as someone he could confide in and depend on looked like a dangerous mistake.

Sidney's core conflicts regarding loss surfaced through PI. He continues to try to defend against what he feels is a dangerous dependency and the threat of losing me as a helper and companion. If he allows himself to need me, he fears his desires will poison me and turn me into a controlling, fragile, and parasitic mother. The moment of loss would be when I, in phantasy, would turn from a loving-mother object into an attacking mother. Life would be supplanted by death, love by hate, and predictability by dread and confusion. He is scared that I would leave him and he would be hunted down by his own rage and despair, now inside me.

Technically, I found it best to focus on his defensive use of PI as well as the specific nature of his anxiety. My focus has been the interpretation of his concerns about loss. My countertransference helps ground me and shows me which way to proceed. Also, his lack of affect has been a useful starting point in showing him how he puts his unacceptable feelings into me for disposal.

CHAPTER SIX

Loss and primitive methods of relating: difficulties in the analytic encounter

Some patients come into treatment and show us, through transference enactments and through gradual working through of their deeper phantasies, that they see most important interactions and close relationships as contaminated in some way by the experience of loss. If we are able to work with them for a while, it also becomes evident that many of these patients have also experienced actual traumatic loss in their early development. This may be the divorce of parents, death of a care-taker, or separation from an important care-taker. It may be in the form of ongoing loss of a protective and trustworthy parent, as in the case of abuse or neglect. In any case, there is often a combination of external and internal experiences of loss and trauma. Analysis shows that the external and the internal influence each other in synergistic ways that often bring about greater and greater states of misery, defensiveness, and anger.

Through the transference and their unconscious and pre-conscious phantasies, these patients show a great deal of oral aggression, envy, spite, and fear of abandonment. Separation and persecution are central, organizing, psychic principles.

These types of patient seem to divide into two subcategories. Some, such as the patient discussed in this chapter, are much more aggressive, narcissistic, and paranoid. The transference is sadistic, demanding, and controlling. Rarely do these patients stay in treatment for very long. Their angry way of relating defends against the internal experience of loss and terrible fear of attack from an object that used to be good and now is bad. In fact, they are identifying with this betrayal and then passing on the trauma to the analyst through projective identification.

Other patients, such as the case discussed in the next chapter, seem to be much more masochistic, dependent, and parasitic in their object relations. These individuals usually stay in treatment but require long and often difficult analysis. They can sustain the rigours of analytic therapy because they have some degree of hope that the analyst will provide what they seek and they do not feel as paranoid or controlled by the treatment.

Overall, clinical work shows that the majority of patients dealing with separation and loss anxieties present with a complex mixture of both sadistic and masochistic profiles. They oscillate between being paranoid and demanding to being meek and parasitic. Their oral aggression is expressed both passively and actively.

"Larry"

Larry was a patient who presented selected aspects of himself to me. We would then relate in a certain way for days or weeks, trying to understand what is taking place. The flavour of our relationship would then shift to another aspect of his personality, revealing other types of phantasies. Larry organized his objects from a masochistic perspective and tried to hide his strong oral wishes to be fed by his objects. One of his primary conflicts had to do with wanting to be fused to an idealized parent who would take total care of him. As soon as he allowed this strong oral craving to emerge, he felt he would be taken over and smothered or rejected, attacked, and abandoned. Therefore, he was usually resisting and denying the closeness he wanted and using a pseudo-autonomy to get by. One compromise was a parasitic, masochistic way of relating in which he made sure never to appear competent, for fear of being judged or neglected. Of course, his masochistic stance allowed him to be secretly aggressive towards his objects and judge or neglect them behind the scenes.

These sessions are of a very narrow nature, in which we were solely involved with his fears of depending on me and his worry that he will burden me. Usually, he was much more worried, aggressive, and competitive. Larry is a patient with whom I find myself in various enactments. These seem eventually to lead us to deeper understanding of his internal world. For weeks or months at a time, he will force himself into a submissive, masochistic stance with me and his internal objects. This defends a more sadistic, controlling, and narcissistic side of him that comes out momentarily with quarrels over schedules, fees, and such. Larry has certainly benefited from the analysis and continues to do so. However, he continues to use splitting and projection to organize his world. Rather than a more typical rapid oscillating style of splitting, he tends to "set up camp" in one aspect of his mind and stay there for long periods of time before shifting to an opposite aspect.

Larry has been in psychoanalytic treatment for ten years. Initially, he came for help with what he termed "relationship problems", but he clearly felt uncertain about most things in life, including career choice, sexual preference, and his sense of identity.

Larry is the younger of two children and told me that his mother was verbally and physically brutal with his sister. From Larry's account, his mother was self-centred, critical, and prone to never-ending lectures. Much of this behaviour was camouflaged within the ideas of "good manners and good citizenship". Larry's relationship with his mother has been extremely ambivalent and quite stormy. He emphasizes her negative qualities and denies the enjoyment and fulfilment he has spending time with her.

Larry's father had a chronic temper and erratic mood. He was a man who felt that things should go his way, telling Larry to have a lemonade stand, a skateboard, and girlfriend years before Larry would ever consider these ideas himself. The experiences that he could have chosen for himself were mandated by the father. Larry often projects those aspects of his father onto me, usually mixed with his own urges that he finds intolerable.

When Larry was 6 or 7 years old, his father was killed in a car accident.

After high-school, he went to college and managed to get a degree in business, despite enormous anxiety and despair about his self-worth. He felt that he was a fake, was "scamming the system", and was taking up space that somebody much more deserving could fill. Several part-time jobs during and after college earned him only enough to pay rent in shared accommodation.

He has had few friends or love interests over the years. When he does begin a relationship, it is one in which the object is idealized and he is devalued. Recently, these roles get reversed.

Larry has moved in and out of his grandmother's home several times over the years. He leaves his grandmother's home to live with room-mates, but always returns in a state of vocational, mental, financial, and emotional collapse. For the last two years, he has lived with his grandmother. His relationship with his sister remains distant and conflicted, fluctuating between envy and disgust.

Recently he said, "To be honest, and this is very hard, I really enjoy being able to live with my grandmother. She makes me cookies and milk. I can stay up late and watch TV. It's so nice to be there with her." In the transference, he protests about being dependent on me and then confesses his desires to "snuggle" with me. Only on rare occasions does he allude to an all-powerful desire to be totally taken care of and fused to me. He feels very embarrassed by this and tries never to discuss it. Part of this wish is his wanting to take care of his dying father getting reversed.

At the beginning of treatment, his conflicts about being "taken over by the establishment", his fears of "becoming just another briefcase-carrying robot", and his disturbing feelings of never fitting into society had left him in a state where the mere thought of getting a job would begin a spiral that usually ended with his being in bed for several days, depressed and hopeless. While the same dynamics still exist, now he is able to cope, manage, and work through these problems much better. These are predominately paranoid–schizoid anxieties about control, abandonment, and attack that repeat through fluctuations of projection and introjection.

Over the last ten years, Larry's accomplishments have included new friendships and an occasional romantic connection. In the last two years, he has dated several women and has kept a steady job. This current job is working out well. He is actually thinking about it as a career, which is the first time that Larry has ever considered such a personal investment into life.

Simultaneously, Larry remains bonded to the phantasy of an object that is angry, self-centred, and ready to reject him. He, in turn, is willing to be in such a relationship in exchange for love and survival. He fears the loss of the object's irritation and disinterest because it would mean a loss of connection. Additionally, his one-step-forwards and two-steps-backwards approach is a compromise between the desire for autonomy and power and an atonement based on the phantasy of enraging his beloved, yet angry object. This occurs in the transference when he feels that his needs overwhelm me and cause me to be drained and angry.

Larry uses splitting to organize his internal world. He longs to be close to me and depend on me for love and attention. He is so anxious about being independent and active that his compromise is to submit to me in a passive stubborn manner. Then, he invites me to push, lecture, and discipline him into becoming an active agent. In this way, he avoids his fears of autonomy by seeing me as forcing him into it. Larry says, " I am scared to do things myself and screw them up because then I would be kicked out, so I do nothing, to be safe." He is frightened of being all alone. He is willing to give up his own identity to avoid losing his idealized object. Therefore, he worries that I will take over his mind and become an internal dictator. He is equally fearful of taking in my interpretations because he might drop them, break them, or use them incorrectly. He imagines that I would be very hurt and angry if he doesn't use my comments in some sort of perfectly optimal way.

At times, he is also rebellious, angry, or sadistic and refuses to take in any part of me. He tries to capture me by acting helpless and making me rescue him, then rejects me as being too pressuring and dominating. Masochistic desperation is used to mask his more aggressive and controlling phantasies.

Larry has explained that he wants me literally to hold him in my lap, do his work for him, make his decisions for him, and keep him safe and close. At the same time, he feels he is pathetic and weak to need my help at all. He wants to be his own man, accomplish things by himself, and pull himself up by his boot-straps. These oscillating feelings lead him to ask me never to leave his side, and quickly afterwards he rejects me as an unnecessary luxury. A recurring variation of this pattern is when he refuses to do anything at all because he feels scared and overwhelmed. Larry will plead with me either to hold his hand and guide him through it or to discipline and beat him into doing it. He then begins to feel that his neediness has overwhelmed me and I have become furious with him and want to get rid of him. At that point, he tries to be a nice and properly behaved little boy and works hard to receive my approval. This leaves him resenting me and feeling that I am a slave-master who pressures him into my image.

Larry wishes to devour, consume, and cling to his object. Con-sequently, he is afraid that he has destroyed the object and is now all alone and overwhelmed. He also feels that the object will return to take him over, own him, or deny him the "food" that he so desperately desires. Then he refuses to receive any part of the object, leaving him starving and empty. Finally, he feels he will be force-fed, yet he craves to be eternally spoon-fed. Therefore, Larry often refuses to chew and therefore chokes on the very sustenance he wishes for.

> P: I don't know what to talk about. I thought of calling you last night. I was so frustrated, upset. I was really out of it.
>
> A: What stopped you?
>
> P: I don't know. The same stuff as usual. I was feeling so stuck in every way, totally unable to move, really screwed up. I was feeling so upset.
>
> A: What was going on?
>
> P: Well, a real combination of stuff.
>
> A: You're reluctant to tell me.
>
> P: It's hard to discuss the girlfriend thing. It's easier to talk about work. I've already put most of the feelings behind me. I had a lot of work due by yesterday, but I totally dug my heels in and accomplished nothing. Actually, I finished one

of three assignments. I blew off the other two. I didn't even go to work the other day. I knew I could get away with it without any direct penalty, but I really wanted not to have any work hanging over my head for the weekend. I planned to take off up the coast for the weekend with my girlfriend. I did do some of the research work to begin the other two projects, but basically I didn't want to do it. I felt so stuck, I went back to bed and watched TV I felt so fucked up, so frustrated. Then yesterday I was late to work. I got there feeling miserable. I was so frustrated and not feeling like I wanted to deal with any of it. I don't feel like I am doing ok. The other workers got their reviews. I got an, "Above-average" report, but most of my co-workers got an "Excellent" rating. It was a confirmation of me just getting by. I am so sick of it but still doing it. I am always off-balance. It is such a horrible way to go through life. I hate how I feel. I hate how I am. Nevertheless, I have to move forward, somehow.

A: You said this topic is easier to talk about than your girlfriend.

P: Yes. We had a nice talk last time, but things got clear about our relationship. She told me she was sleeping with another man. I realized where we stood. I called her later, after I got off work. I felt crummy and wanted to feel safe. She wasn't there. I went home feeling like a real mess. She called me back and we ended up spending the night together. I told her how I was feeling. She was light and happy. It was nice. I felt good being there. So that's how I am right now, not totally depressed.

A: You mean because you could see her?

P: Well, instead of being by myself, instead of being alone and thinking of how awful my life is, I got to see her and not feel so all alone.

A: You wanted to be with someone when you felt so crummy, yet you felt you couldn't lean on me for some reason. You wanted my help but something got in the way, something pulled you away.

P: I feel I have to handle these things on my own.

A: You must be tough?

P: I have never been able to rely on somebody without it being a major mistake. I always expect too much from people, and they are always incapable of giving me what I need. I worry if I push you too much that would happen. If I rely on myself, it will be better, less risky.

A: You save me by managing how much you put on me. You ration out how much you will need me so you don't burden me.

P: That's right. What if I reach out and nothing is there! Yet it doesn't work to rely on myself.

A: You think you will hurt me and I will go away. How are you thinking you do that?

P: I don't know if it's that I will hurt you, maybe it's that you won't care. It's actually both. Yes, both. It's so scary. If I reach out to you, I have to look at my pain and examine it. When I look at it, it becomes real, and who is to say you can really help me. I want some kind of cure, relief, but I am scared to take the risk. My family, fuck! They are worthless in that department. I can't rely on them for shit! I have always felt like my family lets me down, especially when I reach out. Totally useless! My family is shit when it comes to being there to support me if I open up. Shit! My mother should not have been allowed to have children, its criminal. It gets so fucking awful, so scary and stuck. It's my life story, depressed and stuck and feeling like shit. It's always been that way, always stuck.

A: You figure all your needs will eat both of us up and I might not even care to help.

P: That's right. So how is a stupid phone call going to help me?!? Plus, I feel so guilty for bothering you.

A: When you say the "stupid phone call", it makes our relationship sound so pathetic and useless.

P: Well, I feel it won't ever be enough. I would suddenly realize how much I am overwhelmed and then you would say, "Ok, see you next time."

A: Your seeing me as pretty cold-hearted.

P: Well, this is a professional relationship. You're the doctor and I'm the patient.

A: You're worried that if you expose all the terrible things that are inside you I will ignore how painful it is. You will lose me as a helper.

P: I just don't know how you can help?!?

A: Your telling me right now how terrible it is and how scared you are.

P: When I leave here I am on my own. Always on my own. Unless I am lying here, in this room, our relationship is gone. It doesn't exist any more. If I am here it exists, when I leave it disappears. Then I am all alone again, and really scared.

A: How does it happen that you can't take me with you when you leave? I go from good to bad, I leave you.

P: Well, you are pretty formal, I guess it has to be that way. I think there are two yous. There is this one, caring and loving, and then when I leave you are cold, professional, and totally gone. You're just an apparatus, a cold machine.

A: That is a real radical switch. I am loving you and then suddenly I am a cold machine. By seeing me as a cold apparatus that isn't there for you when you feel lonely, you don't have to take the risk of depending on me and possibly losing me.

P: I think I do want to depend on you, but I am worried about the consequences.

Larry struggles with enormous oral neediness and oral rage. He fears it will overwhelm me. He says he worries he will never get enough. At the same time, he worries I will be offended and reject him. I am essentially confronting him on that by first pointing to the reality of our relationship and how he distorts it. Next, I interpret his fear of hurting me and needing too much. To avoid my rejection or attack, he makes a compromise, a mental bargain. He maintains a quiet, masochistic role in which he secretly feeds off me but never breaks the rules of what he feels to be a master–slave relationship.

Next session

Larry missed a session because he was going to an office function, which he had told me about the previous week. He phoned during the time we would have met and left a message saying, "I feel totally stuck, can't find any motivation. I am really stuck today." We discussed this at the next session.

P: I feel so overcome with anxiety. I feel lost.

A: I got your call. You sounded like you were upset.

P: Really? I sounded upset? I can't think of a word to describe how I feel. It was a very frustrating weekend for sure. I felt isolated, alone, scared, tense, stuck, nervous, really bad.

A: You just left a message, like you wanted to get rid of the bad feelings. You didn't want to talk to me in person?

P: I didn't know that was an option.

I am interested in this comment because of the history behind his fear of "bothering" me and the many times his phone calls have come up before. Although he knows I would gladly return his call if he needs to talk to me, he has consistently felt scared that he could make me angry and overwhelmed.

A: I think you know it's ok to ask me to call you back, but you get very worried about using that option.

P: Could be. Why would I do that?

A: It's interesting that you don't recall us talking about that before.

P: I hear you yelling at me, "What the hell is the matter with you!! Why don't you remember, you dumb shit!!"

A: I think that is exactly how you felt when you missed the session. You wanted to be close to me and have our session together but somehow I would turn into an cold machine who would judge you. [*Here, I choose to interpret his perceptions of me, rather than his own decision not to come to the session.*]

P: Yes. I think that is totally right on. It seems like we have identified lots of stuff and I have put the solutions together. But they don't quite fit. It's a puzzle that doesn't fit quite together right. I don't know why I feel so anxious, but I am doing better than the past. Yes, better lately. Work and my relationships are all shitty but I have felt surprisedly in control. Maybe the girlfriend thing has left me feeling out of control.

A: How so?

P: Well, I felt safer in my own personality without it leaking out. But lately, I have been changing. It's a bad sign, little things. I have grown attached to Jane and scared of losing her so I am really nice. But I am not being myself any more. Last week I felt so crummy about my job, and then she told me how she doesn't want to see my any more. When I spent the night with Jane I felt good, but maybe because I felt saved and rescued. I noticed I was really being the nice guy the next day. I changed and I didn't like that. I had planned on going away with her this weekend instead of seeing you but I didn't even want to see her at all. She didn't return my call, that felt really bad.

A: I think you were uneasy not coming to see me and wanted to talk with me, but you got scared. You got scared that you would upset me, so you tried to be nice and polite instead. I think you are probably angry with me for seeming to be so untouchable, unreachable, and ready to reject you.

P: Wow! Yes, that is true. When I do that, get all polite, something starts to build inside me, it's a big backlash of anger. It's confusing and scary to see but it's there. Yes, absolutely, it is there! Anger brings out the nice guy in me.

A: You're scared of me getting angry and leaving you all alone.

P: I can't tell where the line is, where I could start upsetting you. It's impossible to tell. I can't tell when or where you will start to hate me if I burden you. It's so embedded in me, this feeling of you getting fed up and me not knowing when it will happen.

A: How do you feel you burden me?

P: Lots of ways, like, "Oh god, not another god-damn needy patient calling." I guess I could just try and see and if there was a problem we could discuss it. But my first feeling is that people hate me, that they will grow weary of me.

A: I think you are very nervous about hurting me and then me hurting you back in revenge.

P: Yes! You got it doc! So I live in a pit of swirling worries, careful measures, and horrible fears. What a wild fucking ride! Why does it have to be so complicated? But it is so complex and overwhelming. It could take years to completely renew me. It is scary to think of how screwed up a person can be, how disturbed a person can be, and how long it could take to slowly fix that.

A: You picture me so paper-thin, easy to be hurt, and easy to be enraged.

P: The obvious quick answer is that I am that way.

A: Yes, I think that is true. There is another side to it. You are afraid of gobbling me up with all your needs, so you keep quiet and polite, yet suffering in your loneliness.

P: It's embarrassing and humiliating to call and say I have all those problems. I want to be independent. Here in your office, my sanctuary, I can really be me.

A: In your mind I change from so loving to a rejecting cold apparatus, but you are hoping I will stay loving and caring always.

P: Well, I have to go now and I will be on my own. It's time to go and now I will be totally all alone. It's back into the cruel cold world out there.

A: You are challenging me to go with you, almost blaming me for your loneliness. Leaving the badness with me.

L: Well, what do you want? It's very scary out there.

Next session

P: Shit!! I have such crappy feelings today, but not anything like yesterday. I was really in the dump, out of it. Very clear that my emotional state was affecting my cognitive state. I had a report due at work yesterday. I hadn't prepared enough, but much more than usual. I did a little research and felt pretty good. But I couldn't calm myself down and do it, my brain was so scattered, really awful. Maybe it's all the pressure I put on myself to be perfect, comparing myself to all the people I see as so smooth. Maybe I should have talked to you, but I feel I burden you. So, to talk with you I think of how much I bug you instead of what we discuss. Even after being here, it's hard to apply what we discuss.

A: You are so busy worrying about how you hurt me and make me angry that it's hard to take my help in.

P: Yes. I feel so out of control. And since I won't let myself get help from you, even if you magically . . . well, actually that is, what I really want is for you to magically show up and put your hand on my shoulder and say, "Slow down, slow down and let's take a look at what's going on." I felt I was in a hurricane, all these bits of data flying around in my head. So my report was very scattered, fuck. Fuck, fuck, fuck, fuck, fuck! I guess I still feel pretty scattered, got so much stuff going on. Boy! Today I had to get an oil change on my car, call the dentist, and meet with a co-worker about an upcoming project. After here I have to do some research on a report that is due tomorrow. I don't know what to do, and then there is the weekend and my friend's birthday is next week too. Shit! Someone called me to do a freelance project and I have to decide on that too.

A: You make these things sound like horrible obligations, but I figure you probably are scared about each thing and feel all alone with it.

P: Yes I do. The boss I have for the new department is a real jerk. I certainly don't have my old problem of never having anything to do, now. I'm overwhelmed. Then there is my favourite area, relationships!

A: What do you mean?

P: How connecting to people gets screwed up when I try and be nice and relate in certain ways. Like last week with Jane and how bad I felt. All this stuff and then add the "I am unlovable" thing to it and I collapse.

P: You feel you must be a certain way with me or you will be unlovable. Why would I have such strict requirements of you, why would I be so picky?

P: Can't you ask me some easy questions? My brain is overloaded. Let me try and answer with an example. A co-worker and I go back and forth with being friends. I am paranoid that she is frustrated with me and doesn't respect me, so I want to tell her to fuck off and quit being so back and forth, but I think she is actually highlighting some truths about me. I am flaky and out of it much of the time, although she is pretty tense herself. I can work with her on all of it or I can focus on myself and see why it all bothers me. With you, it's uncomfortable because I have to verbalize what is screwed up, like maybe I should just deal with it all by myself. It's odd, because by talking about it with you, I can move through problems, but it's a discomfort when I need you.

A: You think you should be super-independent and work it all out on your own, as if it's your fault and you should clean up the mess.

P: That's right!

A: What thoughts follow?

P: I seem to be missing basic building blocks in life that you normally get from your parents. I want you to show me how to find them.

A: A side of you is scared to call me for fear of enraging me, yet here is a side of you that feels comfortable and close enough to ask for direction. Two very separated and divided parts of yourself.

P: Good point. Oh-oh, I am getting confused, losing it! Trying to think about it is overwhelming, can't do it, caving in, out of control!

A: You try so hard to keep the two parts of you apart and separate that it drains you.

Next session

He had left a late-night message stating, "I am very shaky, not doing well at all, can I see you right away?" I was able to see him the following morning.

P: I felt so scattered, I wanted to come in right away.

A: I think you're still feeling upset.

P: Yes, I am. I am curious what you think I am upset about.

A: By asking me to diagnose you, you avoid telling me what is so painful right now. I think you're in a struggle over sharing yourself with me or keeping all your feelings to yourself.

P: It's interesting, even my breathing is so shallow, my whole body is so anxious. Nothing is going right, that's how I feel. I am trying to keep a lid on a boiling pot that wants to release its rage and upset.

A: Maybe you're worried we can't handle all the rage and upset. Are you trying to protect me from the scalding waters?

P: I don't know. I want to pin my feelings on one thing, like Jane, but I don't know if that is accurate. It could be part of the whole picture, maybe not.

A: Maybe it's a starting place.

P: It's so hard to talk about, so scary to look at. It is so very painful and scary. I feel tormented by everything. I feel trapped and tormented by my job, the pending research projects, Jane, my friends, and all the other stuff I feel out of control about. All the anxiety makes me feel so helpless and freaked out. I am totally overwhelmed and unable to do anything, stuck in a mental pit of shit. I almost think that the Jane stuff is a good focus place because there are so many other soft spots, pits where I fall into and keep falling. I guess I am angry and hurt that she is seeing someone else, I don't know the details. I feel I want to give her an ultimatum, yet I felt so ambivalent about the relationship. I still do, so why do I feel this way? Plus, with an ultimatum I could lose what I do have, so why would I do that?

A: You're angry that you seem to only get the scraps in life, but you're frightened of losing the scraps and having nothing if you protest.

P: Exactly. Yes. I think I will come across heavy-handed, and she isn't exactly a level-headed person. So, I worry I could cause conflict. But I can't keep these feelings to myself for ever. If everything else was going well, would I care?

A: I think you often feel that way with me. That if you say all, it will destroy the relationship.

P: Yes I do. If I have that level of trouble in a place I know is safe, how can I do it out there where I don't know if its safe?

A: Well, in the last week you went from refusing to call me or depend on me to calling and asking for help.

This is a tricky way to put it because I am confronting him on his change in anxiety and action, but he might take it as me encouraging him to call more often. In fact, often he is using PI and splitting to put his desire, curiosity, and effort into me while he then does nothing. In a countertransference enactment of his oral neediness, I then will become overly supportive or active.

P: Hmm, I think I started to accommodate and be nice when she told me she was with someone else.

A: That's when you put the lid on the boiling pot?

P: Yes, I believe you're right. Fuck fuck fuck fuck fuck fuck fuck! . . .

A: That is also part of your hurt.

P: Maybe I am full of shit, but I don't think it's the sex. It's about how I feel. I guess because loyalty is so important to me and I want badly to be loved and cared for, faith and love are connected to sex. I am so insecure and locked into these notions and want to abandon those ideas. I feel tied to monogamy for those reasons, I've always felt I had to be a faithful little monk with people when I had other urges.

A: Maybe you really want a close, faithful one-to-one relationship but you're so scared of it and how you could get hurt that you tell yourself you don't need it, that monogamy isn't your thing.

P: To me that means I am needy and pathetic. Why can't I be close to more then one person sexually? So many of my relationships are based on fears of being alone. The desire to be with someone ends up so unsatisfying.

A: We have talked before about how you may pick women to be with who are unavailable because you're scared of fully being with someone.

P: Yes! I let women pick me and I feel I have nothing to say about it. I feel so lonely and really empty and scared so I want to be with somebody.

A: Perhaps you very quickly size up a relationship to see how you can be the underdog and then you painfully accommodate. With me you very quickly imagined that I am upset with any dependency or neediness that you have, so you try and quickly be polite and undemanding.

P: You know me too well!

Next session

Larry was silent for ten minutes at the beginning of this session.

A: What makes you so quiet?

L (Silent for 5 minutes): I feel very weird. (Silent for 5 minutes) It's just been so intense the last few days, I feel I am just trying to get back to normal. (Silent for 5 minutes) I don't like feeling this way and the way I felt for days now. I am not quite as bad right now, maybe not. No one said life would be easy but it can sure push and pull you around. (Silent for 5 minutes)

A: What thoughts are you having?

P: I am confused and feeling pressured to talk, like I should be discussing my fears and anger. Like I should be a good patient. I just feel really weird today. Good or bad, I can't tell, and I just don't feel I can explain it. I feel on the hot seat.

Guess I am angry and hurt, like a caged animal, confused. I don't know.

There is a cagey, cat-and-mouse-game feel to how he is with me. I feel he is being withholding, distant, and possibly teasing me a bit.

A: I think you're angry that you tried to be close to Jane and then felt like she pulled the rug out on you. Maybe your taking out your frustrations by inviting me to be close to you and then your pulling out the rug.

P: Shit, you're good! Yes, maybe your right but maybe not, I'm not sure. I don't think so, but I don't know.

A: You gave me a complement and then started to take it away.

P: Oh, oh, you're vulnerable. Maybe your feelings are hurt.

A: You wonder if you hurt me, like you felt with Jane.

P: I feel I have merged with Jane, I feel like she feels, it's weird. She seems so tormented and I am trying to sustain a feeling of torment.

A: Interesting choice of words, that you are really working at trying to feel miserable so you can be the same.

P: Oh my god! That's a big one!

Only some of Larry's dynamics are illustrated in these sessions. As mentioned, he and other patients like him will oscillate between various sadistic and masochistic bargains and strategies to deal with phantasies of loss and persecution.

Larry desires to be one with me and to be infinitely cared for. Yet he tries to hide how desperately needy and angrily self-important he feels. Secretly, he seeks an ideal object who will protect him and soothe him. On the outside, he pretends he is autonomous, or, more often, he thinks he can be a slave in exchange for love. Additionally, he worries that if he succeeds in life, he will no longer be eligible for closeness and love.

These sessions represent a slice in the treatment when the issues of loss, safety, control, separation, and autonomy were all played out against the backdrop of phone calls, schedules, and missed appointments.

It would be possible to mistake Larry as suffering from depressive anxieties. He does worry that he burdens me and hurts me. However, he feels he has injured me so severely that it is fatal and that I am unable to forgive, tolerate, or understand his actions. He imagines that I will surely seek revenge and try to hurt him just as severely as he hurt me. It is the loss of me as a good object and my subsequent rage that he is most anxious about. It is the phantasy of me leaving him and attacking him, in combination, that he is most fearful about. This is a paranoid–schizoid dilemma, a primitive eye-for-an-eye rejection, abandonment, and attack.

CHAPTER SEVEN

Maintenance of hope:
the working-through process

The patient discussed in this chapter, Mr X, is much higher functioning than was Larry, the patient discussed in chapter six. Indeed, Mr X is often negotiating the border between the paranoid–schizoid and the depressive positions. However, he still fears he has caused irreparable damage to the object and that the object will seek drastic revenge.

"Mr X"

Mr X came to treatment for help with relationship problems. He was struggling to understand his turbulent relationship with his girlfriend. As with other women he had dated, Mr X felt that he could rescue her and educate her with his superior intellect and talent. After a short while, she became a burden and he didn't know how to get rid of her.

Following an initial evaluation, we agreed on a psychoanalytic treatment: meeting four times a week, using the couch. Mr X had been to several therapists over the years, but never in long-term psychoanalytic work.

His father, as Mr X recalls, was an overbearing, harsh, and angry man who wanted things done his way. He would get drunk and would frequently push Mr X, his brother, and his mother around. He would yell and slap my patient when drunk and generally lecture or scold him when sober. Mr X was told he was a "weak excuse for a man".

My patient describes his mother as a quiet woman who appears very polite and understanding, but is actually very controlling. Mr X says she is passive-aggressive, always getting her way through indirect means. Controlling seems to be a family trait. Some do it outright and others do it covertly, but power is very important to everyone.

When Mr X was 5 years old, his father was shot during a barroom fight. He was paralysed and confined to a wheelchair. He continued drinking and died of alcohol-related complications when Mr X was 11.

Shortly after his father was shot and paralysed, Mr X had begun a variety of obsessional rituals. He had to count things, washed his hands till they bled, stopped riding his bike, and began saving things. He felt unable to cope unless he prayed daily. Mr X often wished his father dead during this time. This made him very anxious, so he tried to undo it with all types of obsessional behaviours, magical thinking, and prayer.

Mr X felt that he had to keep the peace between his parents, respect his father, and make sure he provided his father plenty of quiet for his recovery. Therefore, Mr X frequently tried not to play too loudly and always kept himself in the background. He tried hard to keep everyone happy and healthy. Mr X was an only child, but he had always been very social. Now, he forbade his friends from coming over to play and refused phone calls, as they might bother his father's recovery.

If he had "impure" thoughts, Mr X would immediately confess them to his mother. Angry thoughts, laziness, and masturbation were all sins to tell mother about. All these strange behaviours led the family to take Mr X to a psychiatrist, who gave him medication. This only helped a bit. During puberty, he resumed washing his hands till they bled and constantly confessed his sexual desires to his mother.

When Mr X came to treatment, he worried about hurting me. By being "a man" or doing what he wanted, he thought he would be upsetting me and "asking for it". When he took skiing lessons, he confessed it and worried that I was furious at him for spending money that could go into my pocket. If he were tired from a long day at the office, he would not say so because he felt he was weak and that I worked twice as hard and so he should not complain. Some of these ideas were expectations of us repeating actual father–son interchanges that had taken place over the course of his childhood. However, most of his fears were based more on dramatic phantasies about us in exaggerated father–son stand-offs.

As the years have gone by, Mr X has used me in different ways to meet certain transference needs. He has confessed his sins to me and hoped for forgiveness. This included his sins of purchasing used skis, having fun on the weekend, and wanting to move up in his company. We understood this as his feeling guilty for taking from me and doing things I would disapprove of. In other words, my respect and my tolerance were very important. The more difficult part of these phantasies to get at was his feelings of outright rebellion and disrespect towards me. To hide his greed, aggression, and desire for power, he would emphasize how sorry he was. That way we wouldn't notice what he was actually sorry for. Underneath, he was plotting against me, wanting power and position. But, he feared I would find out and turn from a supportive ally to an angry, punishing enemy.

Mr X was cautious and worried during the first year of treatment. He would make pseudo-reparation by confessing and apologizing to me. Not till the second year did we start to explore his aggressive feelings and thoughts that he erased with reparation, isolation, undoing, and intellectualization.

Diagnostically, Mr X is an obsessional character operating between the depressive and paranoid–schizoid positions. Mr X feels that his aggression and thirst for power harms the object, so he feels guilty and remorseful. However, he also fears great retribution for his crimes and therefore fears his objects and builds elaborate mental bargains to mitigate this threat. He is scared of losing control of the object and is scared of the object's anger, or when he feels that the object is preventing him from getting what he desires. Mr X projects his sadism and envy into the object and then feels alone and persecuted. Mr X makes pseudo-reparation by focusing on how guilty he feels and how terrible he thinks of himself, but this is usually a manipulation. In fact, Mr X uses guilt and pseudo-reparation to hide his sadistic wishes for power and control. His obsessional thinking is often a sacrificial offering to the object designed to make the object think he is truly repentant, while in fact he is still plotting and scheming to gain more control.

These intrapsychic situations result in specific transference phantasies and ways of relating to me. Mr X often tries to control the session by setting the agenda and controlling our relationship with logic and obsessive intellectualization. If I make interpretations that penetrate this defence, he counters by either ignoring me altogether or by telling me I am mistaken. Often, he will tell me that what I am pointing out is simply a normal thought or a normal feeling and that I am exaggerating its importance. In other words, he often devalues me and destroys my knowledge. This envious destruction of what is inside me protects him from realizing that he is not omnipotent. Other times, he will take what I say and twist it around to fit with what he himself wants to think of. Thus, he mentally inducts me as a supporter or loyal follower of his way of thinking. All these acts of superiority save him from the feeling of being with a fading/dying ideal object that could return to punish or attack him.

Recently, he has been able to accept my interpretations of his envy and sadism a bit more comfortably. While sadistic power struggles are common, Mr X is more and more open to my interpretations and more open to allowing both of us to think freely and honestly. At first, he was shocked and angry that I brought up these ideas. For the first year, he assured me that he was perfectly normal in respect of any feeling he reported. By bringing up ideas of aggression or control, I was accusing him of being a bad person. This narcissistic outrage and more paranoid–schizoid stance persisted for quite some time. Eventually, he started to notice his controlling ways and got curious. This occurred in respect to him wanting me to provide him with specific support and understanding, and if I failed I was bad. This new insight was double-edged. On the one hand, he began to explore a more caustic aspect of his personality. On the other, he presented it as a new insight on his part, casting me aside and taking credit. This was an enactment of his internal world.

Mr X is fearful of competing with me as his father and is scared to have more power, more money, and a bigger penis. He feels he is so competitive that he could leave me in the dust. He also feels I would be so lacking in self-esteem that I would feel depressed and threatened by his power. Therefore, his paranoid–schizoid fears of loss are mixed with more oedipal-based depressive fears of competition and control.

We continue to look at these oedipal conflicts and he continues to show integration of these desires and more of a healthy need for autonomy and self-gratification. In other words, we can be different and have different abilities without having to be in an all-out war where one will rule and the other will perish.

Mr X is prone to manic defences in which he devalues the object in order to avoid the guilt he feels for being manipulative and greedy. We have explored his ideas that his identity as a boy and a man were threats to his father's life and that by mentally castrating himself he could not only save his father but look like the selfless hero. Here he again shows the combination of fear, guilt, and his secret plans at conquering the object.

Throughout the second year of analysis, this increased until he became more and more demanding of my knowledge and my "secret ideas" about him. It was as if he not only wanted to possess the breast/penis, but wanted to be one with it as well. He felt more and more excluded from my mind and strove to tunnel his way in with demands and paranoid entitlement. I interpreted this as his wish to be united with his ideal version of me combined with his fear of losing me and my status. I interpreted his fear of driving me away and destroying me with his oral demands. He also tries to control my mind and my status and become one with it. Therefore, closeness, loss, power, and envy play a principle role in Mr X's internal world.

Mr X's desire to know my mind and to control the "secret" areas of my mind are still to be fully worked through. He is not yet able to work on his desires to control the internal couple embedded within me, that he projects into my mind. We are not yet able to discuss his envy of the parental intercourse that he believes goes on inside me.

Mr X uses PI as a method of defence, evacuation, and conquest. He tries to put his intolerable feelings of power, greed, envy, lust, and aggression into his objects. He denies any link with them and then feels unjustly attacked by them. This hysterical way of relating lets him feel justified and righteous about manipulating and attacking others. He uses intellectualization to justify his view of the object now being nasty and deserving of criticism. Eventually, he is overcome with guilt at hurting his objects and then has to double up on his projective mechanisms or find a way to repair the damage. This is usually done with isolation and undoing. As mentioned before, this reparation is not wholly innocent, as he can justify the object needing his superior understanding and help, thereby keeping him elevated and superior.

These processes leave me with various countertransference feelings. At times, I feel bored and numb from his intellectual ramblings. Other times, I feel irritated and ready to criticize him. I can feel in a tug-of-war and in an ideological dispute where one of us has to be right. Finally, I can feel manipulated and conned with kindness and intellectual gibberish. I believe that most of these feelings are the result of a PI process in which I end up having to feel what he suffers with most of the time. Issues of power, caring, and knowledge are constantly brought up, only to be contaminated with multiple phantasies concerning aggression and loss. Mr X brings me into these phantasies and attempts to act out his conflicts with me.

If Mr X feels unable to remove himself totally from the reality of difference and individuality, which he fears and envies, he uses intellectualization to convince himself that he is at least equal to the object, if not better. He intellectually manipulates the object's knowledge and takes credit for it, thereby avoiding feeling humiliated or threatened. Once again, power is important and must be maintained at all costs.

During the first session reported here, he refers to his anxiety about his job. He is applying for a promotion in his company and needed to complete certain paperwork and meet with the immediate supervisor. He has been procrastinating and sabotaging himself in various ways. During the previous session, he had discussed the paperwork he needed to send to the human resources department, which he had left unfinished till the very last moment.

Session 1

P: Ok. We need to figure out what the hell this whole job thing is about! After I came to see you about it, I stayed up till 4 a.m. looking at invoice records and sales figures. Why is it that even while I am such a good salesman I can't sell myself? I keep working below my ability. Why did it take me forever to do a mediocre job? I did the same thing at my last job. I was totally capable of closing all the sales, but as soon as I got to the proposals I shut down. Anything I feel I will be judged on, this happens. I put it off, I procrastinate. Why do I do that? I am glad it's over and in the mail now, but why do I have to do it that way?

A: You are thinking that I must have the answers and you want them right now.

P: Yes, I do. I have a few ideas, but they don't send off any alarms.

A: What do you mean?

P: Well, the judgement thing. I want someone to want me, to really see me as a valuable addition to themselves. So, I must feel pretty bad about myself.

A: While it's probably true that you feel bad, I think you might be saying that to hide how much you want to be a big shot and have someone need you.

P: Yes, you're right. Sure. Even to my first head-hunter, I didn't sell myself very well. I have a history of that. I put myself down just in case. I guess I don't want to be judged.

A: Maybe you get scared of how much you want and how those feelings might hurt someone, so you do nothing as a way of not getting into trouble.

P: Yes, I can see that. I do feel like a greedy jerk. It's like I have an envious, angry jerk inside me who is always wanting more. I want to feed him but I don't because something bad might happen. He could get out of control. I feel so selfish and like a little spoiled brat. I feel so guilty and bad and, like, I must be a really bad person.

A: You are starting to emphasize how guilty you are, like you are hiding your hopes and power behind the guilt. Maybe you think I will get distracted by the guilt and not punish you for wanting too much.

P: Well, I do think I reveal myself to you. I am honest in here. I guess I don't think I am a hundred per cent evil but I am worried that maybe one day I might start feeling superior and better than other people.

A: You are confessing to maybe feeling superior to other people sometime in the future. Perhaps that is easier and safer than showing me how you feel that way now.

P: Ok, all right. Yes, it is true. I am finally willing to admit that to you, but only if you promise to tell me it's not wrong. I am ready to face that side of myself, to admit that I do actually have feelings that are less than savoury. I do have selfish thoughts and see myself as better that other people. It's taken years to tell you that, and it's very difficult. But, I can only do it if you assure me that it's not wrong. I think that these feelings are actually normal and seem natural. I am not sure why you want to bring it up. Why can't I feel that way? What is wrong with it?

A: You're only willing to expose that side of you if I promise not to judge you and even to agree with you that it's normal. You must feel like your running amok and being evil and revelling in it but that I will punish you.

P: Exactly! That is how I feel most of the time. I am a very honest guy. So why do I feel all this stuff?

A: You may be an honest man, but sometimes in your mind you are deliberately controlling me and deserting your father. You are actively doing things to us that you think will hurt us. You're sure you have driven us away and made us angry.

P: So maybe staying at my job in regional sales instead of general manager is a way to be with him and help him?

A: You love him dearly but you also tried to control his life and make him do it your way.

P: That brings up something else. Looking back, I see my father as so stupid in how he dealt with things. He made brainless decisions. I am shocked at how he did so many stupid things, he ended up putting himself in a wheelchair and then in the grave!! If it wasn't for my mother, he would have died right away. No sense. He was just like a little kid.

A: You wanted to control your father and you judge his decisions. Maybe you are still scared of losing him. You think the only way to prevent that is to make him or other people follow your commands.

P: Yes, I am. I am still upset about him. I think this is all the result of listening too much to my mother. She always blames people and points the finger. So, yes. She gets pretty dramatic and judgemental. I guess I can do that too.

A: So you try and control me and your father as a way to avoid losing us or feeling vulnerable and hurt?

P: Yes. (Long silence) So, I need you to give me an example of what a healthy response would be. Maybe you can show me how to avoid that mess and have a normal, healthy response.

A: You are starting to control me to get me to deliver the special secret on how to be perfect and above any emotional messiness.

Session 2

For years, he has been afraid of how dangerous skiing is. He goes skiing, but only to resorts known for their safety records. He is worried about all the big, macho male skiers who could easily overpower him on the slopes and hurt him. He feels that their sense of competition would be so strong that they would probably want to fight with him and beat him up. I have interpreted this as a projection of his aggression as well as his own guilt about success, power, and sexuality.

P: I want to bring up the danger thing we've discussed before. We have discussed my concerns before. I don't know if they are justified or not. Last year, I bought those used skis because I thought it would be safe and economical. I worry about injury and expense, so I want reasonably priced skis that are going to be safe too. So, I don't know if I am overly concerned about money and safety or not. I don't know. It seems normal when you consider the problems that happen on the slopes. Just recently, several people died when they skied into trees. That is nothing to do with equipment, but skill! So, is this neurotic?

A: Given all your statistics, it looks like you're inviting me to debate or fight with you.

P: Yes, probably. The truth is, I would like to be zooming down the mountain on a brand-new snowboard.

A: Lately you are going into more unknown territory with school and the feelings we are exploring. Maybe that is why the safety thing is coming up again.

P: Yes, that is true. But, I think it's a normal thing too. I have to decide if I am going to sell my skis and get a snowboard or not. So, I am just trying to decide what to do, that's all. I need to decide whether to keep the skis or get something else.

A: You are inviting me to be like a parent and suggest a nice, safe, and practical route. You can get my approval by agreeing with that. But secretly you want to be flashy and daring, except it feels unsafe.

P: There is this new snowboard that I would just love to have. It is totally impractical, but it is so cool. It has the best design and so fast and racy. It would be fantastic to just zoom down the mountain with the powder blowing in my face and me making the moves on my board!!. Damn, that would be great!

A: So you were emphasizing the safety issues of your old skis when secretly you're drooling over the new snowboard. It looks like you have to really manage our relationship and make it appear a certain way.

P: Yes, you're absolutely right about that. That new custom board is the perfect ride, and I want it. So, I think I understand. I show you all the responsibility stuff when really I want something very impractical. But the truth is I don't need it. It is impractical. I have so much to do these days. I don't need more projects to get in the way.

A: You're moving away from your wish list and apologizing to me now.

P: Yes, but I don't know what to do. Safety is important to me. It's a normal concern, and the way the slopes are today one has to be concerned.

A: You're scared that you've exposed your more sexy and greedy side to me.

P: Yes, it's all true. I know it's there. I am not denying it. I want all that and more. I don't know. Should I keep the equipment or not? Is it worth it? I wonder if I try and be modest as a way of controlling things and then later complain about it?

A: So you feel powerful and get to feel like a martyr at the same time?

P: Yes. Why the hell would I do that? It's killing me! I have been evaluating myself. Why do I need this conservative lifestyle anyway? I feel an urge to quit my job and take off. I probably won't, but—God! I am all over the map!

A: You're thinking of taking off from therapy too.

P: Well, it's all hypothetical. But, I wish I had more time to myself for fun.

A: You must be feeling captured by your own judgement and wanting to escape, bust loose.

P: Absolutely. I feel I have to do a super one-hundred-per-cent perfect job on everything I ever do. The pressure is horrible, and the result is I never follow through with anything.

Overall, Mr X has made progress in many areas. While certainly not close to termination, he has managed to work with many areas of his conflicted object relations. He no longer has to maintain such stringent control and vigilance over his objects. This is because he is less involved with PI defences in which he disposes his conflicts into his objects. He is starting to look at how he controls himself and his objects and how he fears loss. This is the loss of an omnipotent self-image that protects him from the unknown and it is also the loss of an idealized object. He fears that this loss is followed by rage and punishment.

Mr X had entered treatment because he used women in an omnipotent manner that masked his neediness and hunger for total, ideal love. He used them and quickly tired of them. We gradually saw this as his attempt to cure or save a weak, sickly object and make it wonderful and ideal. This saved him from the pain of feeling that he had lost his idealized love and was now haunted by weakness and self-loathing. Mr X had internalized his father as an ideal object that replaced his troubled relationship with his mother. However, this internal father was destroyed by Mr X's envy, rage, and oral neediness as well as by the external reality of being a crippled alcoholic. There was such a gap between what Mr X tried to maintain in his mind and the reality of his feelings and the actual environment that he had to resort to primitive defensive mechanisms.

Ownership of his anger, envy, and greed and a working-through of loss and mourning are the benefits of his continued treatment. Happiness with his life rather than an obsession with competition and power is slowly possible. As he sees how he tries to force the object to submit to his wishes and how he needs to maintain an ideal image of himself, he feels remorseful and scared. However, integration of these urges and a working-through of these conflicts leaves him feeling hopeful, stable, more relaxed, and confident. Acknowledgement of the truth about himself and the nature of his objects will bring about a healthy mourning process and a gradual integration of identity.

PRIMITIVE LOSS
AND THE MASOCHISTIC DEFENCE

CHAPTER EIGHT

Theoretical issues

Working with masochistic patients reveals a broad spectrum of pathology. These patients exhibit a mix of symptoms and unconscious conflicts that differ widely, yet all converge around phantasies of suffering. The analyst encounters masochistic pathology within both the paranoid–schizoid position (Klein, 1946) and the depressive position (Klein, 1935). The particular anxieties and motivations of these developmental experiences colour and shape the patient's masochistic style.

There are patients who suffer deep masochistic despair and who, upon close clinical examination, prove to be experiencing primitive states of loss, guilt, and envy. Rather than using masochistic compromises to ward off depressive fears, these patients are defending against paranoid–schizoid anxieties.

The Kleinian developmental view

The infant begins life within competing neurological states, psychological and physical tensions, somatic and cognitive sensations, and fluctuating exchanges with internal and environmental stimuli. From the very start, the infant seeks out the object in order to bring about a subjective sense of organization, discharge, and understanding, at first in more primitive ways and later with more sophisticated expression and intent. These conditions of mind and body are innate and, with the phantasies created through complex internal relationships between the ego and the object, make up the emerging substrates of what we term the "self".

The developing, never-static nature of the ego exists in part as the combination of psychological and biological needs and functions of the human organism. These include the countless wishes and fears shaped by aggressive and libidinal forces into complex phantasies. Unconscious phantasy systematizes all somatic and cognitive states. As such, phantasy remains the central fulcrum from which all future experiences revolve in some manner or form.

Phantasy is, from the birth of the organism, the foremost and fundamental organizing, binding, and translating energy of the psychic system. Carstairs (1992) comments on how,

> from the beginning of her work, Klein emphasized the extensive influence of unconscious phantasies on mental processes.—Unconscious phantasies involve psychic representations of instinctual drives which are always experienced in relation to an object.—For Klein, there is no activity, no sensation that does not have an accompanying phantasy attached to it: the baby is a psychological being from the very beginning. [p. 74]

Phantasy states allow for inner aspects of self- and object-mutation. The ego is then able better to give or receive love, defend or attack, move towards or away from the object, and take in or expel. Phantasy allows for adaptation or rebellion to the inner motions of the often opposing and conflictual elements of other self and object constellations. Phantasy allows for inner movement and transformation within self and object representational systems and provides the fuel for this internal motion. In other words, the introjected relationship between the infant and the mother does not remain static: it continues with a life of its own. It is a phantasy state that is constantly being reissued, reshaped, and recreated by both external and internal realities.

Hurvich (1998) states:

> Melanie Klein took the object relations aspect of Freud's libido theory and made it more central, stressing that the internalized good object forms the ego core, and the importance of the object for ego growth. She expanded Freud's conception of the inner world, and described a view of the mind as a stage on which an inner drama is played out, with the players being fantasied objects and part objects. She postulated an interrelationship among internal objects, unconscious phantasies, and drives that has a good deal of clinical utility. Internal objects are seen as the content of unconscious phantasies, and unconscious phantasies are the psychic representations of libidinal and aggressive instinctual drives. [p. 30]

As a fundamental component of psychic structure, phantasy forms the psychic "fluid" through which the organism moves towards self and object connections and away from intrapsychic conflict. Projective identification, projection, and introjection shape the phantasy material and provide for its expression. These mental mechanisms are just as basic and observable as somatic systems, and they operate within a dialectic realm. The back-and-forth nature of projection and introjection parallel more somatic "sets" such as breathing in and out, sleeping and waking cycles, eating and defecating, listening and talking, and so forth. These core mental "sets" slowly shape, form, and individualize the infant's phantasies into what we externally call personality.

Concern and dread

Klein (1937) states:

> We can observe the satisfaction small children gain from their early achievements, and from everything which increases their independence. There are many obvious reasons for this, but a deep and important one is, in my experience, that the child is driven toward weakening his attachment to the all-important

> person his mother. She originally kept his life going, supplied all his needs, protected him and gave him security; she is therefore felt as the source of all goodness and of life, in unconscious phantasy she becomes an inseparable part of oneself; her death would therefore imply one's own death. Where these feelings and phantasies are very strong, the attachment to loved people may become an overwhelming burden. [p. 321]

Klein goes on to detail the possible ways in which a person may cope with this "burden". Denial, displacement, and greedy over-dependence are a few methods she highlights.

When those types of defences break down, the infant is left to struggle with tremendous anxiety. Without a way to get rid of "burdensome" thoughts and feelings, the child/adult is overwhelmed by phantasies of being on guard and protective of the object, of not being able to keep the object alive, and of destroying the object. The many manifestations of this "burdensome" phantasy mostly concern causing harm to the object by either neglect or direct attack. This leaves the ego without the maternal connection necessary for survival.

Both Freud and Melanie Klein influenced the work of W. R. Fairbairn. He constructed a revised theory of the unconscious that also included ideas on aggression. In working with his patients,

> he discovered [that] traumatic experiences in infancy—caused them to feel unloved for themselves as persons. When innate strivings for interaction, especially those based on incorporative wishes, were not lovingly responded to, these infants came to feel that their love was bad or worthless. Deprivation had not only intensified their oral needs but had also imparted an aggressive quality to them, and frustration due to the mother's lack of love had made such patients experience their own love as demanding and aggressive—he conceptualized—aggression as a reaction to frustration or deprivation. . . . [Moore & Fine, 1990, p. 71]

"The mother's lack of love" can prompt frustration and the experience of one's love being demanding and aggressive. In addition, the projection of the persecuted and deprived ego produces schizoid anxiety. On the one hand, this helps to foster individuation and prompts the superego to focus on how the ego impacts the object. This germinates empathy, and the ego begins to monitor more closely its impact on the object, both positive and negative. On the other hand, the infant is not yet sure of his or her power and strength and feels confused about what potential harm or health he or she could create. Issues of caring, guarding, and protection become more important.

The infant, child, and adult all have phantasies within the context of deep attachments to internal objects. These phantasies are given colour by both paranoid–schizoid and depressive experiences. Part of the "burden" of these phantasies involves the feeling of having to endure the attachment for the sake of the survival of both self and object. What formally felt so rich, warm, and secure begins to feel oppressive and stifling. Separation and individuation conflicts and transference struggles over autonomy can often be traced to schizoid anxiety and its derivatives.

These dynamics can push the ego to adopt masochistic defences as a compromise. Otto Weininger (Weininger & Harris, 1983) suggested that a primary masochism can be understood in the light of object-relations theory. He states:

> Just as narcissism can be seen from a Kleinian viewpoint as libido cathecting internal objects (the good breast), masochism can also be understood as the destructive impulse turned—not against the self—but against internal objects (usually the father's penis, the bad breast, or the parental couple in sadistic intercourse, or all of them). [p. 54]

Therefore, the patient who feels burdened to keep his objects alive because his urges threaten their well-being will involve himself in the masochistic compromise of becoming a slavelike, submissive, pleaser. In trying to save the object from the wrath of the ego, the ego actually is betraying the object through small, countless acts of self-righteousness.

The paranoid–schizoid position, projective identification, and masochism

In working with masochistic patients, I have noticed two subgroups. Some patients seem to be functioning mostly within the paranoid–schizoid position (Klein, 1946) and are constantly

defending themselves from phantasies of severe loss and persecution.

Clarifying the nature of the paranoid–schizoid position, Steiner
(1997) states:

> As a brief summary, in the paranoid–schizoid position anxie-
> ties of a primitive nature threaten the immature ego and lead to
> the mobilization of primitive defenses. Splitting, idealization,
> and projective identification operate to create rudimentary
> structures made up of idealized good objects kept far apart
> from persecuting bad ones. The individual's own impulses are
> similarly split and he directs all his love toward the good object
> and all his hatred against the bad one. As a consequence of the
> projection, the leading anxiety is paranoid, and the preoccupa-
> tion is with survival of the self. Thinking is concrete because of
> the confusion between self and object which is one of the con-
> sequences of projective identification. [pp. 196–197]

Paranoid–schizoid loss is the loss of these ideal objects, which are
then replaced by bad, attacking objects. The paranoid–schizoid
world is full of part-objects, distorted by the ego's reliance on
splitting and projective identification. Paranoid–schizoid loss entails the complete and irrevocable loss of the object needed for
survival. This is partly the result of the ego's oral aggression and
neediness that, in phantasy, damages or destroys the object. The
infantile sense of guilt that follows is not from hurting the object,
but for altogether annihilating the object. The infantile ego cannot
conceive of an object that is tolerant or forgiving. It is an eye-for-
an-eye world. Recompense is not possible, and the object demands
perfect allegiance from the ego. This is all the result of splitting and
projection of early unstable ego structure and non-integrated ego
states. Therefore, the ego sees the object as shifting from an ideal
care-giver to a revenge-driven enemy.

In this type of masochistic patient, where paranoid–schizoid
loss is so significant, destructive narcissism and envy play a great
role in internal and interpersonal relating. Here, the ego violently
splits the object and attempts to control, manipulate, and dominate
the object. Excessive and malignant forms of PI bring the ego into
desperate power struggles with attacking objects and fragile self-
cohesion.

Feldman (1997) summarizes the main themes of the PI dynamic:

Klein saw projection as a way the ego had of dealing with anxiety by ridding itself of danger and badness—the psychic equivalent of expelling dangerous substances from the body. But, as we know from the way an infant or young child uses their excretory functions, these may not only be a way of freeing themselves of uncomfortable contents, but also form an important mode of interacting with someone else. These functions can be used aggressively to control, or to engage the other in a positive fashion. Thus, to recapitulate, if we believe that our perception and experience of objects implies a phantasy of the relationship between the object and a part of the ego, then the splitting of objects (at its simplest into good and bad) is inevitably associated with a corresponding split in the ego. Furthermore, the mechanism of projection, by which the organism strives to rid itself of harmful contents, will also involve the evacuation of part of the ego itself. [pp. 120–121]

Melanie Klein, contrary to Freud's views, saw narcissism as a process that developed within an internal-object relationship. She felt that the infant is born into immediate conscious and unconscious relationships to a variety of internal and external objects. These relations are first to part-objects and are often grossly distorted by the infantile ego and its early reliance on primitive defence mechanisms. Nevertheless, the ego is in relation to some aspect of the object from the beginning. The ego captures the object under the sway of intense projective identification and weaves a narcissistic web around it. Then, the ego feels omnipotent and in union with its now captured object.

A relatively new patient, Bill, illustrated these dynamics. He knew I had two offices in different areas of the city. He began his session by asking me if I came to the office we were meeting in only to see him. I asked for details. He said he didn't want to inconvenience me, and if I only came to see him then he was willing not to come at all or to find a way to come to my other office. My immediate feeling was of being controlled and intruded upon. The way in which he tried to "help" me in fact felt forceful and pushy. In other words, this was an act of great sacrifice combined with omnipotence and guilt. I thought he probably liked the idea of having me all to himself and that he was my only patient, meeting in "our" office. He felt like we were one. This massive control and narcissistic bliss felt overwhelming when he imagined that I was taken over by his greed. I thought he quickly tried to resolve this by pulling away. He hoped to make it better by giving me up and going it alone. This self-induced loss probably evoked more oral aggression and envy, and the cycle would repeat.

I voiced my thoughts by saying that he was scared of taking too much of me and that I would be drained and maybe resentful. Here, I interpreted his oral desires, their effects on me, and his fears about my retaliation. He said he was indeed scared about those things and felt frustrated. He said if he stopped coming as a way to save me or went to my other office, he would eventually resent it. He would hate having to be the one who saves the day, "again".

Bill went on to say that much of his thinking is usually about trying to find a way to get me to like him and think of him as a special person who is nice and thoughtful. He said he worries I won't like him and then he "wouldn't know what to do." Throughout much of the analysis, Bill struggled with these phantasies of wanting too much from his objects, hurting them, and being punished in a way that left him abandoned and lost. This fuelled even more envy, rage, and oral desire. In combination, these elements make up a particular type of paranoid–schizoid masochism that involves destructive narcissism.

The relationship of narcissism to masochism

Herbert Rosenfeld (1964) explicated a type of destructive narcissism based on strong omnipotent phantasies. This violent projection and equally violent identification has a manipulative and sadistic motive. Its consequence is to destroy the differences between ego and object and therefore prevent any evidence of individuality, other than the ego's supremacy.

Segal (1969) and Rosenfeld both felt that narcissism is a defence against envy. Segal (1983) made the point that envy and narcissism are two sides of the same psychological dilemma. Rosenfeld felt that the ego's degree of narcissism is in direct relation to the degree of envy. He saw destructive narcissism as a defence against overwhelming envy.

Rosenfeld (1964) states:

> In narcissistic object relations omnipotence plays a prominent part. The object, usually a part-object, the breast, may be omnipotently incorporated, which implies that it is treated as the infant's possession; or the mother or breast are used as containers into which are omnipotently projected the parts of the self which are felt to be undesirable as they cause pain or anxiety. Projection is an important factor in narcissistic object relations. It may take place by introjection or projection.
>
> In narcissistic object relations defenses against any recognition of separateness between self and object play a predominate part. Awareness of separation would lead to feelings of dependence on an object and therefore to anxiety. Dependence on an object implies love for and recognition of the value of the object, which leads to aggression, anxiety, and pain because of the inevitable frustrations and their consequences. In addition, dependence stimulates envy, when the goodness of the object is recognized. The omnipotent narcissistic object relations therefore obviate both the aggressive feelings caused by frustration and any awareness of envy. ... It seems that the strength and persistence of omnipotent narcissistic object relations are closely related to the strength of the infant's envy. . . . The anxiety which is defended against is mainly of a paranoid nature, since narcissistic object relations date from earliest infancy when anxiety is predominantly paranoid. [pp. 332–333]

In my clinical work, I have noticed the link between masochism, narcissism, and envy. Indeed, much of masochistic phantasy and action is based on preventing separation or loss and denying differences. Often, masochistic patients enter treatment because their narcissistic defences have broken down and they are overwhelmed with envy. They alternate between trying to save their objects and raging against these weak objects that imprison them as perpetual helpers. Masochistic patients yell about the people who drain them and always need help, but they cannot distance themselves from them. Without these human projects, their pets, they feel lost and persecuted by their own envious feelings.

Rosenfeld (1988) has written about the link between narcissism and masochism. He states:

> masochism, which I prefer to call sadomasochism because sadism and masochism are so often intricately related. . . . Masochistic reactions are frequently combined with destructive narcissistic structures that dominate the patient, whom they even appear to imprison and paralyze. [p. 151]

So far, I have been describing masochistic patients who are functioning primarily within a paranoid–schizoid experience. A second group of masochistic patients involves those individuals who have managed to develop more whole-object relations. They function within the depressive position. It is helpful to understand the difference between the two types of patients in order to explore the particular anxieties that each faces.

Steiner (1997) describes the depressive position:

> The depressive position represents an important developmental advance in which whole objects begin to be recognized and ambivalent impulses become directed towards the primary object. These changes result from an increased capacity to integrate experiences and lead to a shift in primary concern from the survival of the self to a concern for the object upon which the individual depends. Destructive impulses lead to feelings of loss and guilt which can be more fully experienced and which consequently enable mourning to take place. The consequences include a development of symbolic function and the emergence of reparative capacities which become possible when thinking no longer has to remain concrete. [p. 197]

By definition, there is less reliance on primitive defence mechanisms and a far greater ability to see the relationship to the object as multifaceted and therefore richer and more fulfilling. Rather than the black-or-white issues of life-and-death anxiety which the paranoid–schizoid position can bring, the depressive ego can consider things and people from a variety of perspectives. Therefore, true guilt occurs and separation and individuality can take place. Mourning, guilt, and separateness become painful realities out of which hope, gratitude, and creativity emerge.

Depressive masochistic patients are more concerned about having partly and temporarily harmed their objects. They are able to reflect on the negative ways they impact those they love, and they are not overcome by the day-to-day survival fears of the paranoid–schizoid patient.

Rosenfeld (1988) states:

> It is important to understand that in the depressive position introjective processes are intensified, owing mainly to the infant's discovery of his dependence on his objects, which he has come to perceive as independent and liable to leave him. This increases his need to possess his object, keep it inside, and if possible protect it from its own destructiveness. [p. 166]

Rosenfeld's observations bring out a critical distinction. If the patient is amply fortified with good objects and is not overly aggressive or envious, the protection of the object and awareness of its separateness can proceed relatively successfully. The depressive position serves as a safeguard against envy and destructive narcissism. However, all these hostile elements often block the ego from reaching the depressive position. Rosenfeld (1988) was very clear about these ideas:

> When depressive anxiety can be borne, slipping off into perverse, sadistic, and masochistic perversions can be avoided. . . . I have often observed that when depressive and persecutory anxieties become confused—generally along with confusion of libidinal and aggressive parts of the self—the depressive integration stops and leaves the personality vulnerable to the interfering destructive forces that pull the patient into exciting masochistic suffering. [p. 167]

Here, Rosenfeld is explaining the way some patients who are usually functioning in more mature whole-object relating can regress to paranoid–schizoid masochistic suffering. This is caused by the confusion of libidinal and aggressive states as he discusses, as well as by the excessive use of projective identification in an effort to enviously dominate the object.

The ego's view of the object

I have observed that in both groups of masochistic patients (paranoid–schizoid and depressive), the central wish is for an ideal object that can care for, guide, and teach them. In the paranoid–

schizoid patient, the principle anxiety is the spoiling of the precious relationship to that ideal object as well as the actual destruction of the ideal object. The killed-off object is felt to re-emerge as an attacking, cruel, and needy persecutor. This fear is constantly reformatted and reissued by the various degrees of libidinal and aggressive ego phantasies and the nature of external circumstances. Through projective identification, the ego feels as if a precious commodity (love and food) is taken away. Then, the ego feels hunted down and preyed upon.

The ego bombards the idealized object with demands, hopes, and wishes. Under optimal circumstances, the object is able to "tame" or titrate the ego's hunger into something more manageable for both parties and something more in line with reality. There can be significant intrapsychic problems under the following circumstances: if the ego uses excessive projective identification to rid itself of bad feelings and desires; if the object is unable to contain and process the projections; if the ego refuses to re-introject the containing object; or if the external conditions of life are harsh enough to put undue strain on the relationship between parent and child. In many of these masochistic patients, all of the above are present.

The ego's view and experience of the object is dependent on the ego's level of development and the nature of its current defences. Paranoid–schizoid masochistic patients view the object as a less-than-perfect, fallen warrior who has disappointed, hurt, and deprived the ego of what it needs for basic survival. This phantasy is the result of the ego's intense oral needs, omnipotent wishes, splitting, and projection. Faced with a less than ideal object, the ego is caught in a terrible predicament. To survive, it has to continuously prop up the broken-down, weak object to ensure its own survival. This is a narcissistic triumph but also a horrible persecutory experience. The paranoid–schizoid masochistic patient feels both dictator/master and eternal night-nurse to the object.

One patient, "Norma", summarized these phantasies when she yelled, "She is the mother, she is the parent! Not me! I was the child! When will it be my turn to get attention?" This same patient felt scared that her unquenchable thirst for love, attention, and power would destroy others and bring on horrible rejection. This dilemma would leave her bedridden for days, as she felt so hope-less and lost in the face of such feelings and ideas.

By contrast, depressive masochistic patients struggle with try-ing to atone for hurting the object they love. They feel sorrow and pity for the object. The ego feels it has caused the temporary loss of the object, bringing on guilt and a wish to make up. This desire for reparation is often a catalyst for action. The patient just mentioned, Norma, was unable to function because she could not use repara-tion. The object was gone and she was alone. This felt permanent. Depressive patients have hope that they can make it better and all will be ok again. Ruth Riesenberg-Malcolm (1997) states

> The experience of hope belongs in the depressive position, that is, to the experience with objects felt to be whole, for whom the patient cares and by whom he feels protected. Here Klein's ideas (1935, 1940) about the depressive position are central to my thinking, and help me to understand my patient's difficul-ties with hope. Hope is an affect that depends on the patient's capacity to maintain relationships with good internal objects. He recognizes his dependence on these objects and accepts the fact that they can provide for him. The more secure the rela-tionship, the more capable of hope the person is. If the patient is well established in the depressive position and for some reason or another this relationship is disturbed by hostile feel-ings, which result in attacks on his good objects, the patient will tend to feel guilty. The capacity to sustain hope will de-pend on the degree of his destructiveness and on his capacity to tolerate guilt and carry out reparation. It will also depend on the extent of help from his external object. If this fails, the patient feels that he has lost his good objects and may feel that he has lost hope as well. This leads to despair. [p. 66]

Masochistic patients functioning in the paranoid–schizoid posi-tion have lost hope. They are ruled by the despair of having no recourse for atonement. The fear of loss and persecution is of an all-or-nothing nature and causes sudden and severe fragmentation of the ego. Primitive guilt and loss-without-hope cause reliance on intense and destructive defences such as narcissism. The true guilt of the depressive position prevents a flight into destructive narcis-sism. Depressive loss involves the pain of separation and the feel-ing of culpability, whereas paranoid–schizoid loss brings on an experience of being psychically lost and persecuted. In one the object is lost, in the other the self is lost. If the depressive feelings become overwhelming, the ego may retreat into a more paranoid–schizoid stance, but the knowledge of the damage remains.

Primitive guilt and loss

For masochistic patients within the paranoid–schizoid experience, there is a division, a splitting, of internal relations to the object. On the one hand, there is a feeling of conquering the object (sadistic pleasure) and a feeling of having omnipotent control. On the other hand, there is a feeling of having drained the object with uncontrollable neediness and insatiable hunger. The ego fears that its forceful influences on the object bring dual results: first, the object will be permanently driven away or destroyed, bringing terrible abandonment and loss; then, the object will resurface as an enraged, revengeful enemy. The ego now faces the horror of being hunted down by angry attacking objects while still feeling lost and alone. In other words, there are no allies in this internal experience. In the paranoid–schizoid position, the ego cannot imagine the object as compassionate, understanding, or forgiving, because the ego is not that way either. An eye for an eye is the rule.

Within the paranoid–schizoid experience, there are primitive feelings of guilt—really a dread—over destroying the object. There is simultaneously a great fear and a great loss: fear of the object's revenge, and loss of what is needed for survival (the ideal breast).

In the paranoid–schizoid position, loss and guilt exist, but on a spectrum. Unlike the feelings of guilt and loss found in the depressive position, with the ego's capacity for whole-object relating, the paranoid–schizoid object is in bits and parts. Therefore, everything is in extremes or not existing at all. Reparation is impossible, because the ego has no faith in a forgiving object.

This experience of primitive, unconscious guilt, loss, and persecution has been outlined by Hinshelwood (1991):

> the earliest version of this conflict, however, is not a moral sense at all. In the paranoid–schizoid position the conflict is more over the survival of the ego, which feels under threat of

death. . . . Guilt therefore has numerous tones to it, strung out along the spectrum from horrendous and persecuting punishment to pained remorse, mourning and reparation. At the outset, in the paranoid–schizoid position, guilt is a retaliatory persecution of an unmitigated kind. . . . At first this guilt is persecutory and punitive . . . [p. 314]

Again, paranoid–schizoid loss and guilt entail both loss of the good part-objects followed by their rebirth as deadly enemies. Klein discussed this point in 1935 when she wrote, "the absence of the mother arouses in the child anxiety lest it should be handed over to bad objects, external and internalized, either because of her death or because of her return in the guise of a 'bad' mother" (pp. 266–267).

A common manifestation of masochism, shaped by paranoid–schizoid phantasies, splitting, and projective identification, is the following. The patient seems to seize on an incident or situation with the analyst as something that is unacceptable and intolerable; often, it is something that the patient feels is a burden on the analyst. This is the result of projective-identification phantasies. The patient may begin feeling guilty for paying a lowered fee, asking for special scheduling, having angry outbursts, or always returning to the same complaint. Whatever the trouble is, it is always the patient's phantasy of harming the analyst in some form. The analyst is seen to be tolerant up to a point, but then is seen as pushed to the point of breaking. The patient then wishes to save the analyst from this damage by some offer of personal sacrifice or restitution. However, this leads to deep resentment and wishes for vengeance.

One patient felt so bad for always bringing up her anger with her mother that she thought of reducing her sessions to spare me. Another patient felt so bad about paying a reduced rate that he was going to quit so as to "let me have the space to fill with a high-paying, less complaining patient". With exploration, these patients told me that they would first feel greatly relieved that they would no longer be hurting me. However, they all felt that they would eventually hate me because they had to give up their own needs to satisfy my needs.

What makes these patients different from masochistic patients in the depressive position is the degree of hostility and hopeless-

ness present and the lack of revokability. These patients truly believed that I was being hurt or harmed in a way that was beyond
repair or containment. They imagined that I would be destroyed
by their needs and their imperfections. This is the result of splitting
and the projection of despair, rage, and oral envy. Once battered
and toppled by their hunger, they felt that I would rise up for
vengeance. This is a paranoid–schizoid world where forgiveness
does not yet exist. As a last-ditch measure, they tried to sacrifice
themselves and any of their needs in the hope that I would not
retaliate. This is in the service of survival, not remorse. Finally,
they re-identify with the angry, vengeful object and feel that they
have been robbed. Now, the anger and neediness is within the ego
and again directed at the object. The cycle continues. Primitive
guilt, oral aggression, envy, and loss of an idealized object are
the themes. The ideal object is overrun by the ego's hunger and
neediness. In revenge, a persecutory, bad part-object rises up to
control, attack, and reject the weakened and helpless ego.

Paranoid–schizoid masochistic patients often feel that they are
being forced to care-take their objects. This is based on a very
primitive sense of guilt that comes out of projective identification.
The ego projects its neediness, fear, and dependency into the object
along with aggressive wishes to own the source of much-needed
love and protection. The ego's parasitic envy, aggression, and dependence can be aggravated by an object's less than optimal con-
tainer-function (Bion, 1959, 1962). In other words, a weak external
object may intensify the phantasy of a weak internal object that is
overwhelmed by a hungry ego. Likewise, the phantasy of a weak,
unreceptive internal object can distort the positive container-func-
tion of an external object. Now, the ego sees its object as overpow-
ered, angry, and needy. Therefore, these patients do feel guilty that
they have somehow injured the object and want to nurture that
object back to health. However, they are usually very angry since
they feel that they were "first in line" for much-needed love and
care, but the object gets it first and at their expense! The end result
is a chronic internal dilemma of feeling like the sentry that watches
over a sick prisoner who could suddenly spring up and murder
the sentry. The ego feels at blame that that the object is sickly and
dying. Thus, the ego fears it might be alone and lost because of
its own actions. At the same time, the ego fears that this destroyed

object wants revenge. The result is that these patients often make unconscious compromises in which they will masochistically suffer and serve in exchange for the thin promise of not being abandoned or attacked. However, this creates even more hostility, envy, and neediness in the ego, and a vicious cycle is born.

Again, these feelings of guilt and loss are not depressive anxieties. In the depressive position, the ego feels that it has temporarily injured the object and wants to make reparation. In the paranoid–schizoid position, repair is impossible. The object is not broken, it is destroyed. The ego sets about pretending to make amends while all the time feeling both triumphant and terrified. Often, these patients are involved in a manic state of pseudo-reparation that only thinly hides their sadistic victory over the object and their often psychotic level of fear of being brought to trial for such a crime.

These patients not only project their envy, greed, anger, and neediness into the object, making them fear the object's reprisal; they also identify with a broken down, overwhelmed, leaking container-object that is being cruelly set upon with demands. Therefore, they feel like the suffering, weak, resentful, and misunderstood object that they fear. In a way, this is the primitive reparative effort within the paranoid–schizoid experience. The ego tries to at least imitate the painful state that it feels it has inflicted upon the object; however, it knows that it can never really heal its dying object. This pseudo-reparation is more of a way to appear helpful and to hide one's murderous deed than an effort to truly heal the object. It is a way to pass oneself off as the helpful nice guy while committing cold-blooded crimes.

Envy, and the destructive levels of narcissism used to defend against envy, create a vicious internal cycle. The aggressive urge to own and spoil the object and its contents pulls apart the image of an ideal object. Through projective identification, often of a violent sort, envious anger and entitlement bombard the idealized object, reducing it to a dying or dead object. The primitive guilt and sense of loss is overwhelming. Manic reparation (Segal, 1997a) is used to prop the object up, and the ego adapts destructive forms of narcissism to omnipotently jettison its feelings of loss and fear of punishment.

Masochistic patients wish to have union with an idealized object who will take ideal care of them. This is an object who is independent, strong, and all wise. The ego wants an object that can be selfless and turn all of its affection on the patient's needs without suffering some sort of depletion or resentment. Of course, all external objects, including mother and father, are doomed to fail this unrealistic task. In addition, many patients have endured mothers and fathers who, for a variety of reasons, were quite neglectful or outright abusive. Finally, the early infantile ego is yet unintegrated and easily fragmented. So, when the ideal parts of the ego and its internal object are projected and are then faced with the aggressive, hungry, and demanding parts of the self, this ideal internal object is also bound to fail. If the infant is prone to excessive envy, aggression, and demand and its external objects are less than optimal, there is a good chance of ongoing psychological disappointment. This pain creates even more outrage and demand. It combines with the internalization of damaged and pitiful objects and mean, destructive phantasies about the self. This intrapsychic climate leaves the ego in a severe state of loss. Either the ego will drive the object away, destroy it, and face abandonment or the object will attack and abandon the ego out of revenge. Either way, the needed source of love, nutriment, and survival is gone. Usually, the phantasy is about both occurring simultaneously.

> A 10-year-old patient put it this way. "I know I am a shit and push everyone away, but I don't care because I don't need them anyway. I don't know why everyone picks on me." (*She is depending on denial, devaluation, and manic independence.*) I interpreted that she felt lost and alone because she did away with her object. She said, "Why should I be friends with anyone, including you! Everyone eventually will leave or betray me and I will be all alone. I want someone who is mine from when I am born and then forever. I can't have that, so I will just be by myself. I don't need anyone anyway!" (*She states the ideal she wishes for and how that ideal turns on her.*)

The masochistic patient feels that they have shattered their ideal object. Using narcissistic defences, they feel left with a pathetic, inferior object. This hides the fear of being without an object, having killed off the source of survival, and the fear of deadly reprisal. My 10-year-old patient illustrates this in a striking and sad way. In such a narcissistic state and with strong use of projective identification, the masochistic ego feels that it has ownership of a simple-minded object that cannot care for itself, let alone the patient.

The ego, desperately wanting to be cared for and saved, must try to repair the broken-down excuse for a container. At times, the ego may identify with this broken object and start feeling like the victim. Here, the more direct expression of masochism emerges. Other times, the ego may feel like an omnipotent rebuilder who can guide this poor object and show it "the way". At other times, the ego may feel guilty for having damaged the object and may attempt various reparative manoeuvres. Finally, the ego may feel terribly envious of the idealized union that the object seems to be withholding or depriving the ego of. What is hard for patients to see is that it is often their own greed, envy, or emotional thirst that crumples the object into such a disappointment. So often in treatment, these patients make subtle and martyrish demands for the analyst to be wise and omnipotent and to produce "the answer". If we don't hop to it, they are grossly disappointed and usually retaliate in some fashion.

Projective identification and primitive states of guilt, loss, and aggression lead the ego to envy particular parts of the self projected into the ego. The ego makes an effort to destroy them. This leads not only to feelings of guilt, but to fears of annihilation.

Discussion

Some patients exhibit a pervasive and often intractable form of masochism that upon analysis reveals a primitive fear of loss and a persecutory type of guilt. Their masochism is a desperate attempt to save themselves and their objects from annihilation. These patients experience a paranoid–schizoid (Klein, 1946) form of guilt and loss which involves unconscious phantasies of permanent destruction to the object and extreme danger to the ego.

Working with paranoid–schizoid patients who use masochism as their primary method of relating to internal conflict and to their internal objects presents the analyst with particular difficulties.

These patients struggle with feelings of envy, oral hostility, loss, and primitive guilt. They use destructive narcissism and pathological projective-identification mechanisms to deal with their frightening internal world. In transference and extra-transference phantasies, masochistic patients reveal wishes to dominate their objects and erase any evidence of dependence. At the same time, they feel constantly threatened by an ailing, weak object that they need for survival. They go about trying to prop up that dying object and, in the process, deeply resent becoming a parent to their parent. Masochistic patients, in the paranoid–schizoid position, fear that they are draining the life out of their object and fear that their ideal object will crumble, only to rise again as a needy, angry object looking for revenge. This persecutory phantasy drives the ego to sacrifice itself to the object as a plea for mercy and as a hope to heal this dying, attacking object.

Ultimately, the ego feels enraged at having to sacrifice itself when it really wishes to be taken care of. Therefore, the ego again feels murderous rage. The cycle continues through the mechanism of projective identification. The ego bombards the ideal object with its ravenous aggression, oral demands, and envy. Through splitting and projective identification, the ego divides the object into an ideal object and a weaker, disappointing object. Equally split, the ego is divided into an omnipotent, dominating self and a deprived, overburdened self. Complex conflicts emerge that infest each other to make for ever-deepening cycles of masochism, sadism, loss, persecution, and primitive guilt.

All these factors make for complicated and difficult transference situations. Acting out is common in these patients, and they often bring the analyst into various forms of enactment as well. As with all treatments, it is vital that the analyst find a way to explore and experience the patient's phantasy life about the analytic relationship and about external (extra-analytic) circumstances. Caper (1988) states:

> Infants evoke in their objects, in a realistic and also largely unconscious manner, states of mind that correspond to what they have, in fantasy, injected into them. . . . The analyst acquires transference significance in analysis by agreeing to make himself provisionally suitable as a receptacle for the widest possible range of projections from the patient. . . . [p. 232]

This internal agreement the analyst must make is particularly confusing and difficult to maintain with the masochistic patient. The masochistic patient who is operating within the paranoid–schizoid experience is prone to acting out and to projection of particularly hard-to-contain phantasies and feelings. Caper (1988) states:

> Since an ideally good-part object is felt to be inexhaustible, one doesn't feel that what one has received from it has cost it anything, which means that no gratitude is felt. Likewise, since it is invulnerable, one doesn't feel that anything one does to it will harm it, which means that it need not be treated with respect or concern. [p. 189]

When these sorts of phantasies and perspectives of the object make up the bulk of the ongoing transference, it makes it hard for the analyst to maintain his or her clinical balance. During moments of strong part-object transference, the analyst is tempted to act out feelings of disrespect, grandiosity, power, neglect, or abuse. Understanding the primitive nature of masochistic defences and phantasies helps the analyst regain his or her footing.

Not only will these part-object relationships be projected into the analyst or figures outside the analytic situation, but the patient with also identify with them. Through projective identification, the patient will identify with the object that is always giving and inexhaustible. When the patient's own aggression and excessive oral needs begin to attack the object and overwhelm the ideal object, splitting intensifies and the bad part-object may dominate the patient's phantasies. This is an object that is both weak and dying as well as angry and thirsting for revenge. Therefore, the ego may fluctuate between being the drained, rageful, powerless, and resentful martyr and the noble, omnipotent helper who controls all.

In many ways, the treatment of the masochistic character, whether in the paranoid–schizoid or the depressive position, is the same as the treatment of all other patients. Caper (1988) outlines the concept of transference analysis:

> the analytic management of the transference occurs in three stages. First, the patient projects a piece of his psychic reality—an unconscious state of mind—into the analyst. This is done realistically: the patient projects in fantasy some figure from his unconscious into the analyst, but he also goes beyond fan-

tasy by unconsciously causing the analyst to feel like the projected figure from the patient's unconscious. From the emotional impact of the projection, the analyst may begin to
decipher who or what he is in the transference, what the patient is doing to him, and why he is doing it.

This deciphering or assimilation of what has been projected
into him constitutes the second stage of the analytic manage-
ment of the transference. . . . The third stage of the manage-
ment of the transference consists of the actual interpretation of
it, giving the patient the "food for thought", represented by the
content of the interpretation, and also allowing him to introject
an object that is capable of thinking about his unconscious.
This helps him think about his own unconscious, and thereby
promotes the integration of his conscious and unconscious
minds. [p. 233]

Regarding the practice of Kleinian analysis, Schafer (1997) states:

It is assumed, first, that whatever the analysand says or does
rests on a substructure of unconscious fantasies, and analysis
proceeds by interpreting these fantasies at propitious moments
and appropriate levels. . . . It is also assumed that the analysand's saying or doing anything in the analytic situation implies something about her or his experience of the relationship
with the analyst. . . . Thirdly, it is assumed that rather than
highlighting what is conventionally realistic, adaptive, and
role-appropriate, the analyst's interventions should more or
less subordinate these details to interpretation of the unconscious transference fantasies by showing how these "realistic"
factors are being used seductively, offensively, or defensively
as vehicles or props. [p. 6]

Masochistic patients are best treated by these traditional analytic methods. However, when the masochism is grounded in the
paranoid–schizoid position, the patient brings specific conflicts
into the transference, regarding primitive guilt, oral aggression,
and loss. These occur through the process of splitting and the
vehicle of projective identification. Therefore, analysts must consistently hold their ground and analyse these specific intrapsychic
manoeuvres and the phantasies and affects that drive them.

CHAPTER NINE

Working with
the concrete thinking of narcissism

Masochistic patients test the analyst's ability to provide relief, understanding, and integration through interpretation because they tend to be concrete and situation-focused. Part of this is attributable to the vicissitudes of the paranoid–schizoid position, where much is felt as concrete, all-or-nothing entities that are not linked to one another. Part of this is also the nature of the masochistic patient's internal-object relations and their phantasies that skew perception in peculiar ways.

Paranoid–schizoid masochistic patients often feel ignored, abandoned, or persecuted if the analyst tries to broaden their focus from a repetitious lament to an exploratory curiosity. Looking at the transference will evoke confusion, bitterness, and complaint since they feel that the analyst is blaming them for their problems and not seeing how the world is at fault. These are patients who in one sense claim they are to blame for everything and at the same time refuse to take responsibility for anything.

These patients are continually projecting greed, envy, and hostility into their objects. Therefore, they take our interpretations as recrimination. In other words, they already feel guilty, in a primitive manner, about draining and damaging their objects. They have tried desperately and violently to push these phantasies into the object, so they experience interpretations as a demand to take back responsibility for their crimes. This constant and excessive use of projective identification leaves their ego sterile and lacking integrity.

Klein (1946) made some observations on the difficulties of making interpretations with these types of patients. She speaks to these patient's use of splitting and how the paranoid–schizoid ego puts particular burdens on the interpretative skills of the analyst.

> Interpretations which tend towards synthesizing the split in the ego, including the dispersal of emotions, make it possible for the anxiety to be experienced as such, though for long stretches we might in fact only be able to bring the ideational contents of the anxiety together but not the affect of anxiety. I have also found that interpretations of schizoid states make particular demands on our capacity to put the interpretations in an intellectually clear form in which the links between the conscious, pre-conscious and unconscious are established. This is, of course, always one of our aims, but it is of special importance at times when the patient's emotions are not available and we seem to address ourselves to his intellect, however much broken up. [p. 21]

Here, Klein is describing the technical difficulties encountered when the patient uses excessive degrees of splitting and projective identification, which are common in masochism and certainly the hallmark of the paranoid–schizoid position.

Most patients, including masochistic individuals, present a mix of paranoid–schizoid and depressive wishes, anxieties, and defences. However, the masochistic patient uses the masochistic approach as a central organizer in relating to internal and external objects. The world is viewed and dealt with through that lens. Therefore, the case material I present is grouped around paranoid–schizoid conflicts but certainly shaded by depressive, oedipal concerns.

I demonstrate how I engage with the masochistic patient in the clinical setting. Also, I share the nature of my moment-to-moment thinking in the process as well as what I actually end up saying. It will be apparent that I usually do not say what I am thinking right away, and sometimes not at all. This clinical material is partly an illustration of how I generally work, but more so a demonstration of how I work with the concrete thinking of masochism. Often, I am making simple proposals that link together immediate anxieties with deeper phantasies. The result is, as Klein points out, that at times it is only possible to bring the ideational content together. It is more difficult to access the affect and the phantasies that are tied to that affect.

"Selma"

Selma, a woman in her thirties, felt hopeless and depressed. I saw her in twice-a-week psychoanalytic psychotherapy. She was still in contact with her last four boyfriends and sent them money for their bills. She now lived with a man whom she also supported. Selma was mentally and financially exhausted from serving these men's needs, but she felt unable to stop. She started dating someone at work, behind her boyfriend's back. At first this made her feel better, but quickly she was lending him money and shoring him up emotionally. It seemed she was desperately and completely trying to rescue these men. The thought of not helping them made her feel guilty and depressed, yet she was angry about this "obligation". I had seen her for three weeks before the sessions reported below.

Session 7

P: My friend, the one I told you turned out to be able to listen to me and understand me, is coming out to visit. He called and wanted to know how I was doing. It's weird, he seems to be trying to get close to me now, and that makes me feel like running away. My mother sent me some snapshots and cookies. On one hand, it pissed me off because she seems to deny her part in the whole family situation. But getting those gifts also made me feel like she loved me. I felt funny, uncomfortable. [*She seems not to trust the caring and concern. I am thinking that it is because she gives and loves with such ulterior*

motives that she fears these two people have their own hidden
agendas. I feel she is also wondering about my level of attention and
concern and my motives.]

A: Maybe you want a connection with me but also feel like
   pulling away.

P: Yes, I do, I get mixed up. Like when I start to get what I want
   I go the other way. I think I get scared. I feel, like, without a
   man in my life I would get so depressed that I would stop
   functioning, like the time I tried to kill myself. As it is, I feel
   depressed already, even with a man. I just want to be taken
   care of. [*Here, she is expressing paranoid–schizoid fears of loss,*
   leading to annihilation.]

A: And what do you wish from being with me?

P: I want attention, I want you to take care of me. I guess what
   it all comes down to is that I want love and attention from
   other people. I want to be taken seriously and have people
   respect my opinion. I feel so frustrated at work right now. I
   tell the managers what I think about things, but they totally
   ignore me. I tell them my opinion on things, and they never
   see it my way. Telling them how I feel about things always
   backfires! [*Here, she is using narcissistic defences, projective iden-*
   tification, and oral demands to take back her lost object. It is easier
   to project the blame and guilt into them and feel victimized than to
   feel she pushed them away.]

A: How does it backfire?

P: Well, if I tell them how I see something or how I think something should be changed, they never do it. [*She is showing her*
   need for control and her angry disappointment at not being om-
   nipotent.]

A: So, if you tell someone how you feel and then when they
   don't do it your way, you feel it all backfired?

P: Yes! I just want to be heard.

A: You are saying that if the person doesn't totally agree with
   you, you feel rejected. [*I am commenting on her projective iden-*
   tification efforts to put her anger and contempt into the object,
   leaving her feeling persecuted and judged. Also, I am noting her

grandiose demand to be heard right away in the exact way she wants.]

P: Yes, I guess I am looking for total acceptance. [*She wants the "total" acceptance in order to avoid recognition of separation and difference, which would trigger feelings of loss and guilt.*]

A: Yet we have talked about how that leads to you feeling resentful and wanting something else. You have come to me and want me to be supportive and caring in this ideal way, but I treat you with respect instead. Where does that leave you? [*I am asking how it feels to have to acknowledge our differences and individuality.*]

P: It's kind of interesting. My last therapist gave me all that support and caring, and the therapy never worked. I do want to work to help myself, but I need to find a way of respecting myself. I think I am afraid of rocking the boat. I think that if I really try and make my point known or try and get my needs met, I will rock the boat. I am afraid they would fire me at work and that I would lose my boyfriend. [*Here, she alludes to expressing her wishes and angry feelings, both of which could cause trouble. By showing her hunger, she feels she would be attacked—"fired"—and abandoned—"loss of boyfriend".*]

A: And what would happen here?

P: I am afraid that you would be angry with me. [*That I, too, would persecute her and leave her.*]

Session 8

P: Guilt, guilt, guilt. That is how I have been feeling. Everywhere I look, I am feeling guilty. I feel guilty that I told the guy at work I won't go out with him any more. I feel badly that my mother asked me to visit and I told her that I can't. My boyfriend was depressed and wanted support and I didn't really help him out at all. I didn't really feel like it. The result of all that is overwhelming guilt! [*She feels she has damaged or destroyed her objects by not rescuing them and repairing them.*]

A: The way you talk about these people, it seems they are very dependent and weak and in need of your help. [*I am interpreting her use of projective identification and her conflicts about restitution and restoration.*]

P: That's what it feels like, especially my mother. [*She makes the genetic link.*] She has always been that way, looking for help. She expects me to be there and we can all have these nice fantasies of a happy family. She sucks me dry and throws me away. [*Here, she describes nightmarish phantasies of her mother as a sort of vampire, taking what she needs and throwing away the rest.*]

A: I get the feeling that you see these people as being almost like invalids without your help. [*My impression is that she feels she, through projective identification with her mother, has sucked her objects dry and thrown them away. She sees people as invalids after she has sucked them of what she needs.*]

P: Well, yesterday I felt like I didn't want them to bother me. I was tired of meeting their needs. I don't know how I ever became such a caretaker. I feel like I am always having to do things I don't want to do. I ended up feeling really angry at my boyfriend, my mother, and this guy at work. There was a time where I wasn't so much like this, but once I started dating it all started. I don't know why I always seem to end up being the one that befriends the troubled people, the ones with something wrong. I guess it's when someone feels blue and then they open up to you. But then I end up taking care of them.

A: You have come to me with something wrong and are beginning to open up. How is it to be on the other side?

P: Weird, strange. I feel like I am in the spotlight, I don't like it. I want it to be different. [*She feels more comfortable controlling her weakened objects. With my interpretation, she realizes how needy and vulnerable she is, which means she may or may not be protected by me/object and may even be controlled or taken advantage of.*]

A: How so?

P: Well, like maybe it would be easier if I knew things about you, where you are from, where you went to school, you know, different things about you. It would take the focus off of me. [*These are ways she could begin to own me and gain her control back. She fears we are in a dangerous situation, where I know things about her and could use them to be dominate. She both envies and fears that potential power.*]

A: So you wonder about me and what kind of person I am?

P: Actually I don't. I make it a point to not even think about that, because I would have so many questions. I don't allow myself to think that way. Anyway, this is a place to focus on me. [*She is trying to erase her fears by devaluing and discounting them.*]

A: You say you don't even allow yourself, like you are scared of what would come to mind?

P: I don't know. I just never let myself daydream that far, I stay more in the present. Sometimes I think you might be bored with me or frustrated, but I have told you that before.

A: Those feelings may be yours. [*I think I was too rapid and too general in returning her projection. I believe, in retrospect, that she was starting to fear how dependent and hungry she was getting and that I might get fed up with her for that.*]

P: That's right, we talked about that before. I am angry. Well, it's more, like, irritated at people sometimes. I guess I worry that you really expect me to have something to talk about in here and if I don't you would be troubled. I think about what I could talk about before I get here. I think you would be bothered if I didn't have anything to talk about. [*She is still anxious that I've become angry with her for doing/not doing something to me. She has projected the hungry and demanding aspects of herself into me.*]

A: How would I be bothered?

P: Well, I guess you would get more and more frustrated and eventually just refer me to another therapist.

A: I would be so fed up that I would reject you, get rid of you.

P: Yes, I kind of feel that way when the session is over. I always feel like you are kicking me out, like you have had enough.

It's hard because I have a hard time opening up to anyone and I am talking about stuff in here that I don't talk to anyone else about. So, after I am all opened up, I feel like you kick me out and I have to leave all exposed, like I have a blinking sign telling everyone all about me. [*She is describing the lack of internal protection and the result of excessive projective identification, in which too much is revealed too fast, without time for processing or containment.*]

A: And then they might reject you too?

P: Yes, I have to close up as quickly as possible until the next time I see you.

A: All that must be very difficult. You want my caring and understanding, so you open up and tell me about yourself. But, then you feel I reject you and send you out raw and exposed. [*I am interpreting her phantasy of being too needy and hungry, causing me to be hurt, angry, and retaliating. This is the paranoid–schizoid experience of primitive guilt over having destroyed the object, via projective identification, causing a loss of the ideal object. Then, the object returns in persecutory form to exact revenge.*]

P: I feel pushed around that way. I think you are probably repulsed by me. That is how I always have seen my mother. She seems to be looking for help and love but always ends up being rejected and abused by my father. [*She fills out the genetic aspect: she has identified with a greedy mother who is punished by a rejecting object.*]

A: So you are seeing yourself in her role and me as your father?

P: I think so.

A: Perhaps you are seeing your own wishes to be cared for in all these people you talk about: your mother, your boyfriend, the guy at work, and even myself.

P: That could be right. I do feel like everyone is always asking for something and I never quite get my turn. I do want to be taken care of, but I know I have to find out how to care for myself. I just feel so lost and alone. [*Here, she struggles with a combination of persecutory anxieties—"everyone is always asking for something"—manic defences—"I know I need to care for my-self"—and primitive feelings of loss—"I just feel so lost and alone". The persecutory object is not experienced as a possible source of nourishment, and she takes the stance of not needing anyone. These two internal states leave her perpetually empty and alone—"lost".]*

Session 9

P: I feel so apathetic, I just don't care. I don't feel like taking care of anyone any more. I just don't have it in me. I don't care about it. I have been feeling more and more that I don't want to take care of other people. My boyfriend seems to have all these needs, and my mother does too. She just is always really needy. She tried to talk me into visiting her and I told her no, but she kept asking. I am tired of giving. I don't want to give any more to anybody.

A: I guess that includes me. [*I sense she feels pressured and hounded by her now-forgotten objects. She feels guilt over leaving them and, through projective identification, ends up feeling surrounded by angry and upset objects.*]

P: Well, not really. I just feel like you might be frustrated with me.

A: Are you feeling pressured here? [*I am sure she has projected some of her superego guilt into me.*]

P: You mean, like, I am angry at you? Well, yes, I am. Kind of. Wow. You know, I never thought of it that way. Well, I am a little bit angry that you make me talk and don't just give me answers. I feel, like, you keep the answers away from me on purpose. [*Here, she is showing her feelings and phantasies of me as the cruel, rejecting object that is punishing her for being too needy and greedy.*]

A: Why do you feel I treat you so cruelly?

P (Starts to cry): I don't know. I feel really strange. I don't like telling you that I am angry at you. (Long silence)

A: What are your tears about?

P: I don't know, tears and anger go together for me. When I was growing up there was always lots of anger and lots of tears. It scares me to be angry, I always saw my mother getting hit when she talked back at my father.

A: So you think you are talking back to me?

P: Yes, I worry that you will get angry.

A: That makes it very hard to just be yourself and say what is on your mind.

P: It sure is. I always had to go along with what my father told me. It was his way or else. I think he created a dependency that way. I always had to agree with him and please him. If I tried to say my ideas, he would get angry or put me down.

A: That would make it really difficult to get close to him.

P: I could never get close to him, except by doing what he said. If I ever talked back, he would reject me or worse. [*Here, she links closeness and doing whatever the object demands. Her ideas seems to be, "If I am the slave, I will get love."*]

A: Then telling me about your anger was a risk, like you could lose my attention.

P: I feel like if I rock the boat with my boyfriend, at work, or anywhere, I will get punished. I have to take people's shit or they might leave me.

A: You sound angry about it.

P: I think I am. I have called my last boyfriend a few times a month for four years and he always treats me like shit. If I did what I wanted to, I'd tell him to fuck off.

A: But you don't.

P: I am scared to lose his love or friendship or whatever the hell it is. I don't want to be all alone. [*This is the identification with the discarded, damaged object. The masochistic patient is trapped in a vicious cycle in which the demanding, needy, and weak aspects of the ego and the angry, resentful, and rejecting aspects of the ego—the result of splitting—are simultaneously projected into the object. This creates an alternating, see-saw experience of anger,*]

loss, and persecution. These ego states are re-internalized and iden-
tified with, bring the cycle to full circle.]

A: That is a very powerful idea, that you must be submissive in order to gain love, and if you don't you will be punished or rejected. [*Here, I could have been more present and personal, because it was about us in the transference. I may have backed off in reaction to her previous remarks that "If I did what I wanted to, I'd tell him to fuck off."*]

P: I always have to be the good little girl. I used to dread the last therapy I was in. I didn't want to go, but I felt like I had to. One time she fell asleep on me, and I was so angry.

A: You mean, you told her how you felt?

P: Oh no, I just felt that way. I never said anything, but I quit shortly thereafter.

A: You have mentioned you feel like I make you talk about things, like you have to do something you don't want to.

P: Yes, I felt like I wanted to come to my sessions with you but it is changing a bit. But I am not feeling angry about it yet. [*The "yet" is her threat.*]

A: "Yet." You seem to begin your relationships with emotional investment, but quickly give all the power over to the other person. This was your therapy and now it is becoming my therapy. I am sure that would leave you furious.

P: It does. I hate feeling like I am having to do what the other person wants all the time I am sick of it.

A: So, we can see how you have brought that feeling to our relationship.

P: Yes, I see what you mean. I think I have done that with a lot of men in my life over the years. I want to stop. I have to stop!

A: You want my love and attention so bad that you sacrifice yourself and your own values, but soon you resent how you put me in power, so you want to leave. Leaving scares you because you would feel like you lost my love, so you stay. It is a vicious cycle.

P: I really want to get over this.

This patient felt great envy and scorn for how all her objects needed her. She felt like everyone's slave much of the time and would complain about how she was taken advantage of in countless settings. She resented everyone for acting like a parasite.

Masochistic patients often feel burdened by the demanding nature of others. They feel victims of other people's agenda. With the paranoid–schizoid patient, this takes on a more persecutory quality and a desperation to keep feeding the object what it demands, to avoid retaliation.

The envy that these more primitive patients experience is not so much to do with hating what the object possesses materially. The masochistic, paranoid–schizoid ego primarily envies and hates the emotional ability of the object to need. When the object needs, it takes nourishment away from the ego. The infantile ego does not have hope or trust that there is enough to go around. In the same manner, separation is denied with narcissistic defences so as to prevent the pain of sharing. Phantasies of ideal union are common and are used to hide the painful reality of separateness.

The paranoid–schizoid ego is so reliant on excessive projective identification and splitting that it violently discharges its frustrations and oral demands into the object. This creates an interpersonal and intrapsychic situation in which all the ego's neediness (on a spectrum from desire to demand) are projected into the object. As a result, this clinical material has shown a woman who felt surrounded by needy, violent, hungry objects whom she couldn't respect but couldn't live without. (This internal masochistic struggle with attachment and abandonment is given life with the common quip, "You can't live with them, and you can't live without them.") These were actually split-off aspects of herself that she felt were intolerable. Once in the object, she envied the other's ability to be the way she felt yet was barred from by her own critical superego. Envy pushes the ego to re-own and control the object. However, projection and splitting leave the ego unable to have what is literally a piece of itself. "Why can't I have what everyone else seems to have? Why am I always last in line?" is actually a lament about having lost a piece of oneself through projective identification. The ego is faced with a grisly conflict. The feeling is, "If I have what I want I will destroy my object and then be destroyed in turn. If I project it and give it to you we will both be safe, but then I will envy what you have stolen from me and I will want it back."

"Luther"

Luther was a young man who came for help with feelings of hope-lessness, depression, and lack of direction. He had been in two previous therapies but stopped due to "lack of interest". He said he simply lacked the motivation to continue. I felt he meant he "couldn't be bothered". During the years I met with Luther, we came to see that this "lack of interest" was the result of a subtle, aggressive feeling towards life that resulted in his refusing to par-ticipate. Fear of abandonment and angry entitlement left him, via projective identification, with a phantasy of wanting to be taken care of by a bullying, nagging father-figure.

Luther lived with his girlfriend. They didn't have sex, because of the "pressure" and obligation to sleep with her that Luther felt. So, he often slept on the couch and rarely was intimate with her. Needless to say, this caused tension in the relationship. Luther told me that he had witnessed many verbal and physical battles be-tween his mother and father from his earliest days. His mother, while sounding like a weak martyr, frequently took out her frus-trations by beating the children. On one occasion, she tried to strangle Luther. He claims he bonded much more closely with his mother than with father. To this day, he has a close love–hate relationship with his mother in which she plays the victim and he tries to take care of her.

Luther recalls his fondest times as a child as being with mother alone in her bedroom, sitting on her bed and listening to her complain about her life. They seemed to have a sexualized bond around misery. They took pleasure in recounting the worst parts of the day to each other. An important part of this dynamic was that father usually figured prominently in mother's complaints.

Luther's transference was twofold. On the one hand, he saw me as a wise father. He was a passive pupil of a great teacher who would easily find fault with him. On the other hand, he played the part of the weak and depressed mother and enlisted me to be the rescuing son. In both these phantasies, he was narcissistically controlling his object and then feeling persecuted by it. In other words, he practically demanded to be taken care of and then felt that he would be punished for being demanding.

Prior to the first of the sessions I present here, Luther had left a phone message wishing me happy holidays over the holiday weekend. His voice sounded depressed, and I had the impression he was desperate and wanted to make contact with me. The session began by him telling me how lonely his holiday had been. I chose to bring up the call at that point:

A: I got your message over the weekend. I was struck by how lonely you sounded.

P: Yes. I was pretty down.

A: There seemed to be something you wanted, but couldn't say.

P: Well, I felt alone, and I thought it would help to call you.

A: I think you really wanted to connect with me, to talk.

P: I did actually. I thought it might help.

A: Yet you did it by wishing me a nice holiday. [*A typical masochistic strategy, the idea of "if I give then I will receive". It feels safer than directly asking and admitting to one's own hunger and wishes, since there could be danger associated with direct contact. This is a phantasy of danger to the self and to one's objects. This is created by projective identifications of wanting, anger, and withholding that are passed into the object.*]

P: Yes. I was afraid I would be bothering you, that I would be a burden.

A: Please tell me more.

P: Well, that you wanted to be left alone and the last thing you wanted was to be bothered by me, or by any other patients.

A: You thought you were too needy and would make me angry?

P: Yes. Absolutely!

A: Does that ring any bells?

P: I always felt that way with my father. I wanted to be close to him but, I felt I had to walk on eggshells so he wouldn't be so angry.

A: You take that stance with me too and then feel frustrated that you can't get to me. [*I try to point out how he actively puts a block between us, as opposed to the idea that he is a passive victim of something vague.*]

P: Yes, I do. I think I do that with a lot of people. I do that with my girlfriend and I did that in my last job. I guess I wish they could just understand what I need and then give it to me without me ever having to go through the trouble. [*Here, Luther gives a glimpse of the sad narcissistic demand that is often behind his depressive moods. In general, patients in the depressive position are in a vicious cycle of feeling entitled and demanding but feeling that they have pushed their precious object away and are now left alone and guilty. In the paranoid–schizoid position, they fear that the object will return to exact revenge as well. Survival rather than restitution is the focus.*]

A: Maybe, you see it as trouble because you are anticipating a backlash. [*I feel he imagines his hunger will overwhelm me and I will want revenge.*]

P: Yes, I definitely do. So, I usually choose to do nothing. I think that is one of the reasons I end up feeling so depressed. [*He does nothing to protect the object from his hunger and to protect himself from the object's rage.*]

Next session

Prior to this session, Luther had been reading a children's book in the waiting-room.

P: Wow. That is a really great book, and it is not a big one. Like, I've told you before, I have such a hard time reading things, I don't think I have actually ever finished a book in my whole life. In school, I would just look at them and skim them, but never really read them and understand them. Books scare me, they are too big to handle so I avoid them. It must be some kind of learning disorder, like attention-deficit or something.

A: You're putting yourself in your place. You're feeling you can handle a "small" children's book, but you get overwhelmed by the "big" adult books. [*He is also paying deference to me and staying in the one-down submissive position.*]

P: Yes. I guess what it really is, is that I feel trapped by the big ones. I feel I will never see the light of day. It's a feeling of being pressured and cornered. [*He expresses the depth of his paranoid–schizoid anxieties of being dominated, burdened, and persecuted.*]

A: That sounds very much like how you feel about finding a job. Also, you have felt that way when I ask you to tell me how you feel and think.

P: Yes. And, that is exactly how I feel with my girlfriend. We had a really big fight over the weekend about how committed I am to the relationship. It got really ugly. We were shouting and yelling. I got totally overwhelmed and ran to the sofa and ended up cringing under a pillow. I was really scared, lying there with her yelling at me. She was crying and screaming.

A: It was quite a scene.

P: Yes. It reminded me of how my parents always used to fight and my father would end up retreating to his workshop. They would fight almost everyday. Over and over again. They still do to this day. It was so hard to be around. I always wanted to hide. I still feel crazy when I go visit. I wish I could go back and stand up for myself and make it different. I wish I could change it all. The only problem is that I always feel like I am hurting the other person when I speak up. That is what happened when I tried to be honest with my girlfriend.

A: You do seem to feel like you can easily hurt people with your true feelings. [*I am leaving open the level at which he may be experiencing this feeling, whether it be depressive or paranoid.*]

Pt (Long silence): I am remembering something. Many times after really bad fights between my parents, my mother would tell me to make sure to never be like my father, to never hurt people like he did. I think I feel like my father. I am afraid of hurting other people. [*Here, he seems to indicate a more depressive experience, in that he is able to think of the other person and conceptualize the way he has identified with that other person.*]

A month later

During a session a month later, Luther started off by making a comment about a phone call from his public defender and his parole officer. About two years ago, Luther had finally saved up enough money to buy his first car. Up till then, he had always relied on public transportation. He felt excited about having his own car, but it probably made him quite anxious as well. It would have been a major move towards independence and power. His friend Tony, a drug dealer and known liar, convinced Luther to loan him the car money so he could post bail. Luther agreed under the terms that he would get the money back immediately. All of his friends told him not to lend the money, that he was going to get swindled. When Tony didn't pay it back, Luther seemed to bend over backwards to believe all of Tony's excuses. As the years went by, we would talk about it, but Luther always maintained a stubborn belief in Tony's good character. Even when it was painfully obvious that Tony had no intention of ever paying him back, Luther would overlook it and claim to have no negative feelings about it.

When Tony was going to move out of town, Luther's friends told him that he had better get his money or he would never see it. Luther told me that the "pressure" started to get unbearable, and he felt "emotionally forced" to do something. After asking Tony about the money for several weeks with no success, Luther was getting more and more anxious. This was part of a projective-identification process. I interpreted that he had put all of his anger and motivation into his friends and me. Now he had to re-own it, and it felt like pressure.

The week before Tony was to move, Luther broke into Tony's house. He took all the stereo equipment, the television sets, and anything else of value. He did this in broad daylight and loaded it all into a borrowed truck. He left a note for Tony saying he had done this and would hold on to the property until he got his car money back. Tony called the police, and Luther was arrested on a charge of breaking and entering. This was the first time that Luther had ever broken the law—indeed, he had been a model citizen in every way.

Luther told me that he felt desperate to do "something". Interestingly, about a year before, he had told me that his ultimate phantasy was to be locked up in jail or prison because it was the perfect combination of being taken care of and being told what to do. I had interpreted it as a phantasy of having perfect love and attention for being the slave and victim and it was a way to atone for the crime of wanting to be strong and assertive, which he believes hurts those he loves. He said he would love it if he was ordered to do what he should do, because he never feels up to doing it himself. I pointed out that he was describing his relationship to me.

When Luther's girlfriend came to bail him out of jail, Luther wanted to stay and said he liked it there. Several correction officers and his girlfriend had to persuade him to leave.

Prior to this session, Luther's probation officer and his public defender had called to ask why he wasn't following the court's recommendations for community service.

A: You seem to be giving up on your court agreement, and this would put you back in jail.

P: If I don't get immediate gratification, I give up. I have been thinking of exercising and all about it. But I know I won't do it. I have been thinking about my career, or lack of it. There is just something in the way of me ever progressing, getting better. I feel like I am giving in and there is something that pulls me down, something that always keeps me from proceeding.

A: You see failure as the best option.

P: I have really low energy, so slow. I just can't get moving. I think that accomplishing things feels like a punishment, and so I don't ever want to do anything. I am just plain lazy.

(Silence) I can't even remember what my point is, I don't even know what I am thinking about. [*The internal equation of success = punishment seems to stem from his fear of leaving mother and breaking their masochistic bond.*]

A: Maybe you were thinking of something in the silence that you want to get rid of, not remember. [*I wonder if he feels that thinking is equal to success as well, so he tries to destroy and project any evidence of mental self-agency.*]

P: I was thinking that you're judging me. Like maybe you're sick of me or thinking that I am pathetic. I know I've told you that before, but here it is again. Like you think I am lazy and that you're probably pretty tired of hearing me complain. I feel pretty anxious about how my life is going. I feel I better do something, that I need to do something! But I don't want to.

A: Maybe you think I am pressuring you to do something and you're feeling I'm pressuring you. To deal with that, you are digging in your heels and saying "no way"! Then I will pressure you even more.

P: I like it that way because I feel like I am getting helped. I can see myself doing that sometimes and I am disgusted with myself, but I ignore it. I need people to feel sorry for me.

A: You said you want help. It sounds like you are really after pity.

P: My father used to judge me, he still does. I feel guilty too. I think about getting a little job somewhere, but then I feel I would just end up feeling obligated and overwhelmed.

A: You're reluctant to build yourself up since you think you would lose all this help and pity.

P: I agree 100%! Yes. That is it exactly. But, I do try, I really do. I actually do try!

A: You seem to be inviting me to judge you and say, "try harder"!

P: Yes, that is on the money! You're right!

Luther continues and tells me several stories that all end the same. He tries to do something to better himself or take some form of assertive action. Then, he is either disappointed in someone or someone takes advantage of him.

P: So, why should I ever go through the trouble of trying in the first place? It seems so hopeless. I just am sick of trying.

A: I take it you're pretty angry about having to engage in life, to participate.

P: Well, yes, I do. But I feel really guilty too. My brother always helped my father out. They would work together while I stayed inside with my mother. I would always be willing to help other people, but not my father. I ended up feeling like I should be with my mother, helping her. I felt obligated to take care of her. I felt guilty not being out there helping my father, but I really wanted to be with my mother, helping her to cook and clean. I liked it better. I felt much more comfortable doing that.

A: I think you have taken on the punishing, angry way of your father and the meek and resentful way of your mother. You are those ways with me now.

P: I never said much to my father, never talked back, because he was just "doing his time", like a prisoner in the marriage. So, I could never just be his son.

A: He felt trapped and obligated too, and you didn't want to burden him any more.

P: Exactly.

A month later

P: I couldn't make it to the last session, because my father wasn't feeling good. He had to go see a specialist for his stomach. He has always had problems with cramps and aches but this was something more serious. He was in a lot of pain. They are going to do a bunch of tests. There is no prognosis yet, but the doctor said he has a workaholic lifestyle and that could be giving him too much stress and causing stomach problems. Maybe it's like ulcers or something.

A: You're worried your father is hurting himself just like you hurt yourself. [*I refrained from interpreting that he feels he has caused his father's illness.*]

P: I think I want you to feel sorry for me sometimes. I have been doing lots of stuff lately. I have been keeping busy and doing little work jobs here and there. At first, I really didn't want to do anything. But then it got better. My brother's problems with the law suit are starting to ease up so I feel less worried about him. He has such a hard life.

A: You have compared yourself to him in that respect. [*I am wondering if he feels he has to wait and let everyone else get better first before he can succeed.*]

P: Yes. My girlfriend says my whole family tries to be a victim of life. She says we are all total victims.

A: What are your ideas?

P: Well, I certainly copy my mother's victim role in life so I can cope better and so I can manipulate things. It's a sense of power. It works sometimes. I get angry when it doesn't. I can't seem to deal with ordinary life, I break down under the challenge. I only look at the immediate rewards, not the long-term consequences. I have to go meet with the probation officer, but I don't feel like it. I keep talking about getting a job, exercising, or taking a class, but I never do any of it. I don't know. My girlfriend has been on my case for spending too much money on partying and drinking and being lazy. I don't bring in any money, so she is upset. I know I should do something but I can't figure out what to do.

A: Maybe you are really just refusing to do anything.

P: Yes. That way, I get to have the other person be my parent. They get angry and tell me off and tell me what I should be doing.

A: You seem to enjoy that, to need it. You push me to be that way.

P: I expect it. I don't know why I am like that.

A: You are like your mother, a victim, and you want me and other people to treat you like your father treated her.

P: That is exactly how I am! Poor little Luther, he just can't do anything! Oh, poor me! Its hard to fight that. It's like a tape I keep playing. I feel so sorry for myself.

A: Do you feel you're able to manipulate me into being like your father?

P: No, you're too tough. You don't feed into it too much. It's frustrating, I have to do the work. Actually, I was going to wait to the very end of the session and ask your permission to go to a party instead of my next session. I was going to make up a sad story to get you to say yes and not be upset with me.

A: You're trying to manipulate me with a soap opera to avoid getting me angry. By acting weak and passive with me, you actually are pretty powerful and controlling.

P: Yes. I am starting to see myself doing that more and more. Usually, I don't notice it till a lot later. But now I am seeing it when I do it. I usually do this stuff on autopilot. I expect to be punished, like I am trying to get out of something. My father is the same way. Sometimes even though I know I am doing this stuff I will go ahead and manipulate it and do it. That way, I don't have to risk a stressful situation. I can't tell sometimes, it gets all mixed up. Being honest or direct is too much work and I don't like work.

A: If you picture me as angry and ready to judge you, it would be easier to not be direct.

P: Yes, I don't want the violence. It's much more soothing to get the pity. I like the immediate gratification of the pity. I feel forced into the corner if I have to look at the big picture. I don't want to. I like it here when I have to manipulate to get my way.

Next session

P: I have been thinking about various careers I could get into and thinking about what I would have to do in each one, but I never really follow through. Essentially, I haven't been doing anything for a very long time. I feel so unfocused. I lose interest in bettering myself. I feel dragged down, depressed. I just want to stay in bed.

A: You're noticing how resistant you get.

P: Well, there is so much idle time. I need to do something. Everyone tells me I need to work. Maybe they are right. They look at me as if I am lazy, but I don't want to commit to anything.

A: You seem very committed to doing nothing.

P: Yes, I feel like I don't contribute.

A: What about the part of you that rebels against me and tries to manipulate me?

P: I hate that part of me. (Long silence)

A: What are you struggling with?

P: The injustice. I feel I have been so wronged. I deserve to not work! I don't want to be told what to do!

A: But, you are surprised when I or other people confront you on it.

P: Yes, absolutely. I am so in it I don't see it. When they tell me something about it, I resent it. I feel like a kid who is told he has to go to bed because he is too tired. I feel it is not right, just not right! But, I guess I will ultimately have to get some kind of job.

A: You sound uninterested and bored with the idea.

P: Yes, that is exactly what I feel. I want the easy way out, I don't want to have to do the work. Maybe part of me wants to try but I am glued to my bed. I feel so depressed.

A: Seeing me is a form of work. I think you fight me just as hard.

P: Of course. It's agitating and frustrating.

A: So you fight back, resist, and try to not engage.

P: Yes. My girlfriend knows I do that too. She says the money for therapy is going to waste if I don't try and work at my problems. Why am I so meek, lazy, and slow?

A: I see it as more of an active hostile action against me and against our relationship.

P: Yes, that is what it really is. It used to make me feel guilty. I never used to help my father either. I would stay in bed or hang out in my mother's bedroom.

A: Maybe you erase the guilt by acting like a victim.

P: Well, yes. But I do feel like a victim. I don't want to succeed. I feel so much despair.

A: What do you fear you will lose if you change?

P: I would have to give up my freedom. I feel so stuck.

Next session

P: I started looking for a job. I actually called about one! It didn't work out, but it was good to see what is actually out there. The first time I look at an ad, I usually feel very different from when I look at it later, a second time.

A: Something in your attitude?

P: Yes, I think so. I almost blew off our session today. I was thinking about going for a ride in the country instead. Also, if I don't have it right in front of me, I forget. Maybe it's because it's for me. Maybe I see therapy like school, like it's an authority thing.

A: Part of you likes to rebel and play tug-of-war with me; another part feels meek and powerless. I think you relate to me like a victim to hide the fact that you're ready to play hookey.

P: Therapy is like taking medicine. As soon as I feel better, I stop taking it, even though I am supposed to take it till the bottle is finished. I do better if someone else tells me what to do. I don't like to have to make myself do things.

A: So, you want me to command you and tell you what to do. That way you feel close and secretly running the show. Ultimately, you resent the person for doing that to you.

P: I would like it if you reminded me of each therapy session, to tell me when I have appointments. I would be somewhat resentful, but I would like it. Do you think I will ever change that?

A: Only if we can understand what excites you about getting me to order you around.

P: If I don't get my way, I get really upset. My girlfriend is starting to really get on my case for that. I set people up to see me as a victim.

A: . . . And then to get angry with you.

P: I can't stop it. I don't know what to do, I can't seem to find a way out!

A: By acting weak, you demand my attention and care.

P: Yes. And I block out the helpful stuff, like what you tell me. It's a way of staying the same. Maybe that is why I forget to come to my therapy sessions sometimes.

After six years of treatment, Luther has made great changes. These have been internal and interpersonal. He started his own small business, which is doing well. In most of his relationships, he is able to deal with people directly and honestly. Instead of passively demanding and threatening his objects, he is able to find ways of negotiating his needs and accepting the object's point of view. While he still has the urge to be the poor little slave to a weak father and a controlling mother, he is able to catch himself using that approach.

Luther's own words best sum up this difficult but ultimately successful case. He told me he feels a nostalgic pull to be the old way at times, but now he realizes the rewards of being different. He sees the old way as a con-job he does on himself to work out problems that are better faced directly. This is painful, but honest and fruitful.

CHAPTER TEN

Transference
and countertransference

While experiences of paranoid–schizoid loss and primitive guilt certainly occur without masochistic overtones, paranoid–schizoid loss and guilt easily engender a masochistic dilemma and promote masochistic strategies for escaping overwhelming feelings of loss and persecution. In discussing primitive masochistic patients, Betty Joseph (1982) states:

> My impression is that these patients as infants, because of their pathology, have not just turned away from frustrations or jealousies or envies into a withdrawn state, nor have they been able to rage and yell at their objects. I think they have withdrawn into a secret world of violence, where part of the self has been turned against another part, parts of the body being identified with parts of the offending object, and that this violence has been highly sexualized, masturbatory in nature, and often physically expressed. [p. 455]

This description sheds important light on the type of countertransference that the analyst may encounter with paranoid–schizoid masochistic patients. Indeed, my countertransference with these patients' endless laments and sadistic complaining is often

"Either shut-up and keep your complaining to yourself or just go and tell so-and-so off, but quit bothering me about it!" This strong internal reaction is exactly the result of what Joseph points out. The patient feels assaulted, in a very persecutory and abandoning way, but is unable to respond in any meaningful way (a way that would create psychic meaning.)

The infantile ego feels unable to withdraw because it will be alone and unable to survive. It also feels that standing up to the object would bring on terrible reprisal and annihilation. Therefore, a crude compromise, or internal bargain, is reached. A cruel, masochistic relationship with pain and suffering is established. This allows for a sadistic/dependent attachment to the object. However, this creates even more envy, hate, and helplessness.

"Juan"

This vicious oral cycle was evident in my work with a patient, Juan, who would avoid any type of thoughts that directly linked us together, for it triggered more envy and longing. He said and did things that showed his desire for a seamless union with me, while at the same time avoiding any evidence of contact or reliance with me. He demanded that I, and others, pay close attention to his every need. This session occurred in the fifth year of the analysis.

P: We have the same haircuts now. [*He just had his haircut.*] Can I open the window? [*This is a request he has made many times before. I have made interpretations through the years about his conflict of wanting us to be the same, as one, but feeling suffocated by our closeness and wanting "some breathing room".*]

A: Yes. Why do you need to today?

P: It's so stuffy, I need some air. I feel claustrophobic. I don't know what to talk about. What goes through my head doesn't seem very important, I guess because it doesn't make sense. I don't know.

A: You have a lot of energy about something that you say is so unimportant.

P: Well, I was upset with myself last time because I was so out of it, I never really settled in. I don't want that to happen again tonight. I had a hard time telling you about work, when I really needed to be discussing it with you.

A: I think you wish to share yourself with me, and you also feel like withholding parts of yourself from me.

P: You got a problem with that?! I don't even know what you just said. I was just being flip. I don't know.

A: You don't want to have a connection with me in your mind.

P: Really? I don't know. It is so hard to focus and be in touch with myself. I can't quite grasp what I am feeling or thinking, and everything seems so fuzzy and unclear.

A: You try to hide certain parts of yourself from me.

P: My mother asked me how my day went, and I got so pissed at her, really angry. I was upset when she went to spend a few days with a friend and never called to wish me luck on my new work project. It is so typical of her and my whole family, absolutely zero support. Now she has tried to make up for it but it's so phoney. At least it seems that way. It really makes me furious.

A: You were angry that she left you and wasn't the perfect kind of mother you wanted, just like you worried we would be pulled apart over the holiday. You were angry that I wasn't going to be there to take care of you properly.

P: Yes. It's getting better, but yes. It is still there all right. I feel so conflicted with it all.

A: You want me but you reject me too.

P: I am not done complaining about my mother. It feels tragic that it's like that. My sister called her recently for some advice on whether to take a new position at the bank or not. I was stunned that she did that, given how cold and shitty she is when it comes to giving us what we crave, the warm love. I really blame her, but she must have had some problems of her own to have gotten that way, stuff I don't fully understand. And then there is my mother and father! What a pair they were. I am left with all the fallout. I feel so ripped off.

My feelings seem so outside my reach. My whole family tells me that this is all my mental problem when I bring any of it up. I feel I must have lots of problems still, especially if I am going to therapy five times a week, but when I look around I see some pretty fucked-up people. The managers at work always yell at each other. This one in particular seems extremely disturbed. [*He talks for ten minutes about how terrible work is.*]

A: You seem to be inviting me to be miserable with you. You hide any moments of competence or excitement from me and ask me to just be gloomy with you.

P: Yes, it's true. That is the big question, why do I do that. There was this nice moment today at work where it all seemed to be ok, but then it turned into something shitty. I tried to hang on to the hope that it could return. That seemed to help a lot. But, normally, I can turn gold into crap really fast.

A: It's a bit of a mystery as to why you would enjoy dragging me down with you. We are on the sinking ship together.

P: I think it may have something to do . . . I don't fully know, but maybe something to do with the basic anxiety I feel. I feel I have absolutely no control so I try and focus on the negative to really be able to show how terrible I feel.

A: You try and convince me and bring me evidence of how bad you feel.

P: Yes. I really need to step up to the plate and ride the pony. I need to start to live life. I am so tired of how it has been for so long. I try very hard and it is getting better, but I don't know. This is my fucking life and my fucking job. I want to be fully invested, and I really want to be doing a good job. My job is so much harder when I don't try. I just make it worse.

A: You made a point to fake your feeling most of your life. You are an expert at finding the sorrow in life. More and more, you are trying to also show me the other sides of you, except you get scared one of us will end up hurt or rejected.

P: Absolutely, that is right on. But I get so terrified. I tell everyone I am ok when I'm not.

A: You often play a bait-and-switch con game with me—you tell me you are totally doomed and helpless, and then, when you feel you've seduced me to rescue you, you say you're fine and independent and don't need my help at all.

P: I know, I know. I can feel myself searching for the pain, looking for the negative.

This patient is prone to paranoid–schizoid fragmentation and shifts between currents of destructive narcissism, masochism, and envy. Betty Joseph (1982) writes:

> This type of self-destructiveness is, I suggest, in the nature of an addiction of a particular sado-masochistic type, which these patients feel unable to resist. It seems to be a constant pull towards despair and near-death, so that the patient is fascinated and unconsciously excited by the whole process. [p. 456]

"Robert"

The masochistic's hidden excitement and the seemingly irresistible pull towards despair makes for difficult treatments and rocky countertransference. Joseph (1982) goes on to say:

> a powerful masochism is at work and these patients will try to create despair in the analyst and then get him to collude with the despair or become actively involved by being harsh, critical or in some way or another verbally sadistic to the patient. If they succeed in getting themselves hurt or in creating despair, they triumph, since the analyst has lost his analytic balance or his capacity to understand and help and then both patient and analyst go down into failure. At the same time the analyst will sense that there is real misery and anxiety around and this will have to be sorted out and differentiated from the masochistic use and exploitation of misery. [p. 449]

Here, Joseph highlights the particular countertransference impasses that occur as well as the importance between manipulation of pain and genuine suffering.

Robert was a patient who illustrated these points over and over in the transference. He had a way of presenting stories about various crises in his job, with his family, or with his girlfriend. While he portrayed himself as the innocent victim every time, each story had something in it that made me think, "Now, wait a minute!" I was constantly invited to jump in and point out that in fact he was the culprit in each episode. Robert managed to get me to become critical and lecturing, off-balance analytically.

He would manipulate us into the same sort of situations. Around scheduling or billing, I would get pushed into feeling judgemental, like a scolding parent. Robert would predictably react with a "Who, me?" innocence. This was a set-up for me now to be the mean parent falsely blaming the poor innocent child. Through the years of treatment, he gradually revealed the sadistic pleasure behind the "Who, me?" He relished playing the naive little boy who had no clue he was doing wrong, while really enjoying a perverse hostility behind the scenes. As Joseph points out, we often had to separate the real misery and suffering he endured in his internal and external life from this masochistic perversion.

Bit by bit, we were able to discover some of the core motivation in his masochistic endeavours. Robert crafted countless sadomasochistic adventures in the transference as a way to keep us locked together. This was a complex intrapsychic bargain with his internal objects. He "locked" us together with a feeling of power, cruelty, and revenge. Having us together prevented loss and abandonment. It also invited me to attack him with judgement and dominate him with confrontations on his manipulations. However, he felt that he was at least in charge of this punishment, which felt better than being attacked and abandoned without any warning.

It was a long and difficult analysis, but ultimately successful. He gradually gave up his masochistic manoeuvres and dealt with the paranoid fears of my attack and rejection. This led to a slow and painful mourning process in which he dealt with the loss of an ideal mother who could take away all his suffering. Robert was then able to take responsibility for the internal and external ways he tried to hurt and manipulate his objects when he didn't get his way. Segal (1997b) writes:

> An infant under the sway of omnipotent phantasies creates a world based on his projections in which objects in the external world are always perceived in the same way, since they reflect

and embody the subject's own primitive phantasies and parts of his projected self and internal objects. They are rigid and repetitive because they are not modulated by the interaction with reality, hence the repetition compulsion described by Freud (1920). [p. 80]

Segal is describing patients functioning in the paranoid–schizoid position. This is the type of repetitive, compulsive distortion of relationships that Robert was in at the beginning of treatment. As we worked through his acting out of these rigid internal outlooks, he experienced life from more of a depressive mode. Slowly, he came to a more integrated sense of himself and of those around him. His relationship to himself and others became whole.

CHAPTER ELEVEN

Grievance
and the paranoid–schizoid experience

Some paranoid–schizoid masochistic patients are so immobilized with rage, loss, envy, and primitive guilt that they make for near impossible transference blockades. They have a profound sense of grievance which can manifest in different ways. This grievance is a direct result of intrapsychic experiences—phantasies—of loss and persecution. Spillius (1997) states:

> I have found that in cases of grievance and impenitent experiencing of envy, defences are used not only to maintain and enhance the sense of grievance, but also to evade acknowledging the acute pain and sense of loss, sometimes fear of psychic collapse, that would come from realizing that one wants a good object but really feels that one does not or has not had it. Feeling perpetual grievance and blame, however miserable, is less painful than mourning the loss of the relationships one wishes one had had. [p. 154]

Spillius goes on to elaborate the link between loss, envy, and masochism. Regarding the defences against envy, she describes one way envy is hidden behind masochism:

[There is] a form of masochistic defence in which the individual feels himself to be omnipotently hopeless, so that the envied object, who cannot cure the individual's despair, is proved to be worthless. [p. 155]

Here, Spillius is describing masochistic patients, who dig in their heels and refuse to take in the analyst, to take responsibility for their own feelings, or to admit their own progress. "I won't" is the battle-cry. One such patient would bring me endless tales of tragedy and failure. Only by asking many questions and examining my countertransference closely was I able to discover his secret success. He in fact was improving in many areas over the course of treatment but would rarely reveal it. He tried his best to keep me convinced that he was an impossible case and that we both should give up hope. He expressed his grievance by forcing me to be supportive and encouraging and to counter his "I won't" with a "Sure you can!" He forced me to hold the hope and dreams of what he could be and what he could have, while he banged the drum about what he didn't have. He invited me to feel as most of his friends eventually felt—an angry reaction of "Quit whining and just do something". This validated his grievance that no one was ever understanding or compassionate, just as he felt his parents weren't.

Core feelings and phantasies of grievance and "keeping score" are very much in line with what Freud (1916) described in his paper on the "exceptions". The chief difference I wish to highlight is the experience and expression of grievance. As Freud points out, there are some patients who loudly and directly claim the right to special treatment, based on a feeling of prior deprivation. I see this as a step towards the depressive position in that the ego is demanding reparation from a hurtful object. Clearly, it is done in a persecutory, demanding manner, but the general idea is that something can be made right.

Masochistic patients functioning more in the paranoid–schizoid position are unable to formulate this reparative demand. They may want to take back what they feel was taken from them, but to do so is inviting annihilation. The paranoid–schizoid ego fears that this type of demand or entitlement would trigger retaliation from the object, leading to abandonment and then attack. Sometimes these patients will split off these fears of loss and persecution into the analyst and adopt a righteous, entitled stance. The analyst's countertransference of anger, impatience, or hate, in reaction to these projections, is a valuable indication of what direction to take interpretatively.

"Melissa", a borderline teenager, found countless faults with her family. She would try to provide any and all types of help, advice, and assistance to her parents because she felt they were unskilled and "pathetic". Melissa felt that they asked for help much of the time, and when they didn't she promptly offered so that she wouldn't have to "clean up the invariable mess" later. She was projecting her own strong oral needs and insecurities into them and feeling burdened by them in return. Each time she tried to force her opinions onto her parents, she was told to mind her own business. This led to terrible fighting and her feeling unappreciated for her hard work to help out her "ignorant" parents. "I told you so" was one of her battle-cries. Over the years, I felt that Melissa was a terribly worried and very hostile lifeguard who would forcibly rescue people who needed no assistance. She would then feel furious for going out of her way and only getting grief in return. Through projective identification mechanisms, this was also the nature of the transference, only reversed. I ended up feeling that she always asked for help only to yell at me for "bothering her" and "trying to control her mind". It was difficult for her to discuss the hatred and dependence that she felt for me. In other words, she hated the feelings of need and dependence for me and tried to blame them on me via projection. In the transference, she felt a dual connection to me, both life-affirming and deadly. She would tell me that secretly she felt very helped by seeing me and couldn't imagine functioning without me. She could see the rewards of treatment, but letting me know was like admitting a nasty sin. On the other hand, she felt that I constantly picked on her and persecuted her by trying to manipulate her mind. This was a projection of her own aggressive, exacting, and intrusive self into me. She would then feel that treatment was a vicious cycle of me hunting her down and her trying to fight back and

prove her innocence. This was part of her grievance. This grievance fragmented her internal connection to me, and she felt a
sense of loss of me as a safe ally and instead had to deal with
me as the enemy. As a result of splitting and projective identification, I became a bad object.

Caper (1988) has described the internal process whereby such in-
tentionality is created:

> Internal objects are formed by the two-stage process of project-
> ing one's loving or hating impulses into an appropriate exter-
> nal object (thereby bringing it to psychological life), and then
> introjecting this object. . . . The bad object differs from a frus-
> trating object by virtue of its having acquired intentionality: as
> a result of the projection of the infant's hatred and destructive
> impulses, the frustrating object is imbued with the psychologi-
> cal qualities of the hating part of the self. It becomes not simply
> frustrating, but destructive, hating, dangerous, and malevo-
> lent. [p. 174]

Over the course of several years, Melissa improved and felt
much safer and happier in life. She started to take responsibility for her own feelings and needs rather than attribute them to
others. This signalled the entrance to the depressive position
and deep feelings of loss and mourning. Bit by bit, she told me
how she felt totally shut out of her family and their love. She
told me how she actively fought to manage and control her
family with her "help" as a way to ensure that she would be
included. She was convinced they didn't want her, so she had
to try desperately to force her way in under the guise of being
nice and helpful. Her progress showed in the transference by
how she was able to let me and my interpretations in, instead of
always shutting me out. As she felt more accepted and
mourned the union with an ideal object, she could let me in and
see that I wasn't always bad.

Another aspect of masochistic grievance within paranoid–
schizoid functioning is what I call the "exceptions to the exception". This is a denial of desire and a denial of grievance. Freud
(1916) explored the "exceptions", those who felt entitled to special

treatment based on feelings of prior deprivation. Some primitive masochistic characters secretly desire special favours but outwardly display the opposite. By denying any needs or desires for special care, the ego protects the object. When the ego feels capable of draining and destroying the object, it can defend by erasing any evidence of hunger or need. So, the ego feels that it is safe to receive in a passive manner, but dangerous to actively take. Patients who are overly compliant, polite, and willing to wait for what they want often have a motto of "I am so fortunate and lucky." These are the cases that always try to help to heal their friends and family, putting everyone and everything before themselves. In the transference, they will quickly and anxiously deny any urge to possess, compete, or conquer the analyst's internal supplies. In fact, through projective identification, they will place their more active feelings, aggression, and wishes for specialness into the analyst.

This projective-identification situation creates difficult counter-transference feelings. The analyst can feel and act aggressively supportive. The urge is to tell the patient, "You deserve it, go for it!" In other words, the analyst ends up full of the patient's urge to be active and to pursue love and ownership of the object. One danger is that the treatment becomes a more suggestive counselling, with the analyst urging the patient to pursue gratification through acting out. Worse, the analyst may start to dominate the patient aggressively with so-called support and advice. The treatment can quickly turn into a sado-masochistic relationship with the patient digging in his or her heels and being passive and the analyst demanding that the patient claim what is rightly his or hers.

The masochistic patients who present as "exceptions to the exception", who proclaim that they need nothing and are far from special, are exhibiting a pseudo form of gratitude. Klein (1957) discussed the outcome of the depressive position as full ego integrity, an awareness of impacting the object (leading to reparation), and gratitude for the object's love. Envy directly erodes and destroys this feeling of gratitude. In masochistic patients in the paranoid–schizoid position, they use a pseudo-gratitude as a defence against knowledge of how envious and ravenous they feel towards the object. Thus, these patients will tell the analyst how grateful they are for the treatment and how much better they feel already. This can be the theme after only the first three or four sessions. They will be overly thankful in a way that triggers uncomfortable countertransference feelings. The analyst will want to confront this syrupy falsehood but will feel fearful that the patient is completely unaware of it and be offended. Again, this is the projection of the patient's hostility and the patient's fear of connecting with the object. At some point, it is helpful for the analyst to interpret the patient's desire and fear to enter the object and claim what is felt to be rightfully his or hers.

Finally, these exceptions to the exceptions have commonalities with those more narcissistic patients who openly demand compensation and special recognition. Both are orally aggressive and want to possess the property and contents of the object (love, knowledge, power, security, etc.). However, both are always reluctant to take any action in or outside the treatment towards that goal. Therefore, it appears that they refuse to get better and feel entitled not to make progress. In the final analysis, this is because of a pervasive fear of abandonment and loss, followed by attack and annihilation. These states of ego fragmentation set the paranoid–schizoid masochistic patient aside from the more whole-object related depressive patient. The depressive patient is mostly scared of having temporarily harmed the object and wishes to make restitution. One is a world destruction phantasy with no hope of survival for either party, the other is a more hopeful "let's make up and make it better" world-view.

"Veronica"

Veronica was a middle-aged woman whom I saw twice a week for one year. She came for help with sorting out her "miserable life" and to figure out why she was always in a "dysfunctional relationship". These sessions are from the last month of her treatment. Rather than providing a case history, I feel that these verbatim case notes give the best picture of who Veronica was and the internal struggles she suffered.

P: Here is a cheque towards my bill. The insurance finally sent something.

A: Thank you.

P: I have been really stressed lately, overwhelmed really. It's about my boyfriend. He is really in debt, he has major money problems. I told you how he ran up my credit cards for about $10,000 and I have to pay it off now. Well, that isn't anything now. The more I got to know him over the years, the more skeletons he brought out of his closet. Legally, he now has debts of over $15,000 for one thing, but that would great if it were the only thing. When he was in his twenties, he spent time in prison and has to pay restitution of over $17,000. Altogether, he is now $60,000 in debt! I feel so badly for him. He has turned a new leaf and has been living a good life for years now but his past has returned to haunt him. I feel like my debt is meaningless, and I just wish I could think of a way to help him. I feel compelled to help him out, even though I can't see how I could. I am so stressed out about it. [*I sense a combination of her wanting to get her grip around this man and her feeling scared that she is so greedy, ready to devour his debt and him with it. More on the surface, I think she also fears he will leave her if she doesn't save him from her grip.*]

A: You sound desperate, as if it is your problem and you want to take it on right now!

P: I feel that way. There has to be a way out.

A: That desperation goes beyond being concerned for your partner—you seem to feel desperate for yourself.

P: Yes, I do. I feel like it is my mission, my duty, to fix this problem. I need to be needed! It is weird, I almost like the crisis times.

A: You suddenly have a purpose, some sort of meaning in life?

P: Yes, it is really strange but I feel like the worse the problems get the closer I feel to him. I think it is a relationship of dependency. I need him, and somehow the problems help. That is crazy, I must be really sick.

A: You do seem to have a relationship with these problems more so than you have a relationship with him as a person.

P: That is right, I have no idea who he is. The one thing I know is how to have a relationship with problems and how to be dependent. There doesn't seem to be much else. [*Here, she is pointing out how she tosses him aside in favour of his treasure: the problems she can own and feel powerful with, in the spotlight.*]

A: Perhaps this focus on problems and dependency saves you from the trouble of having a more real or intimate relationship with someone. [*I made a very off-target remark. In fact, she is being extremely intimate with her object, although in a highly aggressive manner.*]

P: I have always been dependent. It is just like my mother. God, I swore I would never be like her. She was pathetic that way. I have been dependent on everyone, women too. It is familiar. I am scared that if I stop being dependent things will change, my boyfriend might leave me or not like me any more. I can only see negative things about changing that.

A: With all the problems that are occurring with your boyfriend, I have yet to hear any negative feelings; as a matter of fact, you very quickly dismissed his debt to you as meaningless. I am surprised at the lack of any negative feelings. [*I am interpreting her hidden rage at the weak and undependable nature of her objects.*]

P: Well, I am angry that all these skeletons are coming back to haunt him. I see what you mean though, I am not thinking of me at all, only how I can bail him out. Oh my god, that really is exactly what my mother does. She is always catering to my father's bullshit and never thinks about her own needs at all. That always made me furious. She is just so spineless that way. I really need to be needed. If I can get them to need me, then the deal is done.

A: That is similar to how you told me that part of you felt that I just wanted your money and your hard work, that I somehow needed that from you. You're picturing me as not only dependent on you but also quite hostile.

P: Yes, it is like that. I guess I do that with most people. I try and find out what they seem to need, and then I provide it so they want me and need me.

A: You use dependency as a way to control and stabilize your world, and when you can't you feel desperate and inferior. [*I comment on the phantasy of loss that is involved in her sado-masochistic relating.*]

P: I do. I am good at it. If they don't need me, they won't want me.

Next session

P: I feel so frustrated. I am not doing well. The more I look at myself the more shit I find, and it is disgusting. Everywhere I look there seems to something wrong with me, and it feels like therapy just shows me how I am messed up. I am left with this big pile of crap, and I don't know what to do with it. Therapy seems so slow, and I know it is crazy but I feel angry at you for it somehow. Of course, all of this makes me want to stop coming. I just feel like I am getting worse instead of better. [*She is demanding that I give her positive attention, and she is frightened I see through her Mother Teresa approach to people.*]

A: You have very strong expectations of yourself, and they are spilling over onto me.

P: I always judge myself very harshly. I feel like I am a weak person; I have always felt that way, weak and stupid. The more I am in therapy, the more I see how I do all this self-destructive stuff and I am disgusted. I want to go back to being in denial about all this, it is easier. I feel overwhelmed.

A: Your increase in self-understanding feels offensive?

P: Well, I just have to look at all this shit now. It seems therapy wants you to see this stuff and then hang out with it. I can't do that, I want to fix it now, do something to change it quick and get over with it. I just see how pathetic my life has become and I have no respect for myself, none at all. [*Here, she is realizing her hostility and her effect on her object, which scares her and possibly brings on guilt feelings.*]

A: You keep bring up this idea of respect and weakness.

P: I think it goes back to my mother. She was never able to respect herself at all. She took so much shit from my father and never stood up for herself. She didn't respect herself and my father surely didn't respect her. She was always so damn weak. I really respect women who are strong and capable in this world, I look up to them. I guess I couldn't look up to my mother. [*She is full of hatred for her less-than-ideal container-mother.*]

A: Maybe you wanted to.

P: I did, but she never provided any kind of decent role model.

A: In some ways she did provide a negative role model that you seem to have internalized.

P: I see what you mean. God, it disgusts me to think I have turned out like my mother. You know, it is strange. Lately, I have felt less anger or hatred towards my mother and more towards myself. Somehow she seems to be not so bad, but I am much more unhappy with myself.

A: Perhaps you are angry at the mother side of you.

P: Maybe. I am so used to judging myself that I don't know any different. Sometimes I have an idea about something or I find myself doing something and I reflect on it. But then I am instantly criticizing myself. It changes so fast.

A: Perhaps these things are connected together. You have a difficult time knowing the difference between your feelings and other people's feelings, and your useful knowledge can quickly change to useless judgement.

P: My mother seemed to take great pride in being the perfect martyr. She could do that job well. She took all the abuse from everyone in the family and seemed to be happy in that role. We talked about how I am hanging on to my role of fixer and victim, maybe that is the same thing.

A: You have commented before on your wish to be a martyr in all your relationships.

P: Exactly. I feel like I want the problems fixed now! The idea of waiting seems strange, painful. I want it to get better now! [*She is showing her hunger and desire to possess all.*]

A: I can't help but wonder if that is how you may have felt at times as a child.

P: Well, of course! I hated it, I wanted it to be different, I wanted the family down the block—not mine. There were always some sort of problems and nobody ever fixed them. I can't stand to look at this stuff, my life is a nightmare. I feel so damaged, like such a fuck-up.

A: It is intriguing that you start off investigating yourself and finding out information and then you begin to judge yourself and label yourself.

P: Yeah, but I was totally aware of it as it was coming out of my mouth. I knew I had started to change like that.

A: So you are on track with that, you are able to observe yourself.

P: Now that you feel better about me, that I am on track, I can feel better about myself.

A: You need my validation to feel better?

P: Yes, I think I do.

A: Again, I wonder if you confuse your feelings with others. I did validate you, but you had already spoken of your own victory. I was following up on your own validation of yourself, yet you gave me total credit. [*She is projecting her dangerous victory into me and then demanding it back, with envy.*]

P: I see what you mean. I think I do that with a lot of people; I don't even realize that I have those positive feelings about myself. I ignore them and wait to hear them come from the other person.

Next session

A: Here are your bills.

P: Thank you. I will have to wait till like Thursday to give you something; I am having a really tough time right now. I am even short on my rent at this point, but hopefully by the end of the week it will be better.

A: What is happening with your finances?

P: It's really terrible right now. The job is always really slow this time of year, my rent is really high, and I am having to cover the minimum payment on the credit card that my boyfriend ran up. It has been really slow at work, so I haven't been making minimum hours. When you fall below a certain level then you have to pay for the insurance yourself, and that is another hundred and something dollars a month. My rent is really hard to handle this time of year too. I used to have someone sharing my apartment so it was cheaper, but she left. It is a really nice place, but right now it is hard to manage. I feel like I don't know how I got myself into all this. I am actually feeling some resentment towards my boyfriend over his complete irresponsibility. He went from being a compulsive drinker to a compulsive gambler to a compulsive shopper, and I am having to pay for it. I get so angry sometimes that I start thinking maybe it would be better to write it all off and walk away. I can't do that, though, because I don't know where I would be, all alone. I resent what he has done to me, but I don't want to create a rift in the relationship. I am the only one with any money. We can only rent movies on the weekend, because I refuse to go out and spend money on us. [*Here, she punishes him and controls the relationship.*]

A: It seems you have a great deal of control over him in that sense.

P: Me? I don't have any control, I usually feel taken advantage of by him.

A: By letting him create a massive debt to you, he is very much accountable to you.

P: God. I have never thought of myself as in control. That is too weird.

A: You have mentioned that you depend on people being dependent on you. In that sense, you are dependent on being in control of others.

P: That is just too strange, I feel sickened to think of myself that way. You know what picture is coming into my mind. My father was always like that, he would make sure you were dependent on him. Oh my god, he would do it with money. He would give out money instead of love and have you be dependent on that. I can't believe I have ended up being like my father.

A: Maybe it is hard for you to give out something real of yourself, as it sounds like it was for him. [*In this comment, I am leaving open her possible motivation, whether it is an aggressive withholding or a fearful distancing.*]

P: Well, I don't think he was capable of giving anything, he was so fucked up. I had this dream the other night and it was strange. *I was a cocktail waitress and I went over to my friend's home. Her family was seated at a dining table in their driveway. They ordered drinks and I went inside to the bartender and as soon as we laid eyes on each other we were wildly attracted to each other. We began making out. In the distance I could see my last boyfriend.* I woke up and felt repulsed, like I was cheating on my boyfriend. I think I don't feel satisfied in the relationship right now, but how could I think these kind of things?

A: You say that as if you are a victim to the dream and to your own feelings. It seems you were very much in charge or in control in your dream.

P: Well, I see what you mean. You know, I hate to say this but that is a lot like how my mother is. She is weak in a manipulative way. God, I can't believe that I would end up like my parents. I can see how I do have my boyfriend by a leash and the people at work too. It just sickens me to see myself that way. I just keep flashing on a picture of my father; he forced us to respect him, but the result was that we hated him. [*When she begins to make the genetic link, it borders on an evacuation of responsibility into them, a blaming of them. However, she is still maintaining some self-reflection.*]

A: You want respect too, but you fear you won't get it unless you sacrifice yourself. Ultimately, you force the respect out of the other person.

P: Or out of myself.

A: Good point.

Next session

P: Here is a check. It is all I have right now. I am really stressed out about money, I need to talk to you about this. Maybe we have to meet less until I am doing better. Things are so bad right now. They have never been this bad before.

A: Tell me the details.

P: Well, as you know my rent is really high, and this is the worst part of the season at my job so I am having really shitty days there. Some days I don't make anything. I don't even have all my rent money yet. By Thursday I hope to be able to give you more of my balance, but it is getting bad from all directions. As you know, my boyfriend isn't in any position to help; as a matter of fact I have to cover his bills, so it makes everything that much worse.

A: What are you doing about that?

P: What do you mean?

A: Well, you are in great need of money right now and he owes you money but isn't paying it.

P: I have tried. I have asked him for it but he always has some excuse. I try and get him to pay me but it is no use.

A: You make yourself out to be so powerless.

P: I am, I don't know what else I could do. What am I supposed to do? I have tried asking for it and talking about it but he just doesn't have it. I don't want to rock the boat, I guess, I don't want to make too much of a fuss. Maybe it would be best to come less until next month, when I will be doing better.

A: It is interesting that you are thinking of ways to reduce what you benefit from instead of dealing with the problem.

P: I tried to deal with him, but I told you it is useless. It feels like you keep asking about him and the money, and I think you must be doing that because if I could get him to pay up then I could pay more money to you. So you want me to deal with him so you can get paid.

A: Rather than see me as being supportive of your struggles, you see me as being just one more person who is giving you a hard time.

P: Well, not really. I just wondered about why you keep focusing on my boyfriend and me. I mean, I know I should just demand it, but you seem angry about it. Believe me, I have really tried to talk to him about it. If I do keep coming twice a week and have to owe you the money, I would feel really uncomfortable, like I would owe you, emotionally. You might want something from me. It just wouldn't feel right.

A: I think you are worried that if you owed me money I might be angry and feel ripped off, like you do with your boyfriend. I would feel like I don't get my needs met and others do, which is your struggle.

Next session

P: I am kind of tired today. Let's see where to start. Oh, after last time I went home and talked with my boyfriend and told him how I felt about being last in line to get paid, and evidently someone owed him some money and he gave that to me so some of the bills are covered for the month. I was glad to get it. I mean, I was relieved of course, but you know. I felt guilty about getting the money, like I put up too much of a stink. I am angry about the whole situation, but it is hard to be angry.

A: I think you are furious about it but have a difficult time expressing it directly, so you use other avenues.

P: Like what?

A: Well, you mentioned guilt for one.

P: I see. You know, the only person I really feel comfortable getting angry with is my mother. I can get angry with her and not feel guilty at all. I don't know why that is; maybe because she just takes it. She deserves it, though, she is such a victim and never does anything to help herself out. I have been angry at her for a very long time. Recently I have thought of writing her a letter telling her how I don't really blame her for my problems and that she probably did the best she could and to not worry about me. I do need to take responsibility for myself. [*Here, she seems frightened at hating her mother and rushes to erase her hostility.*]

A: You were talking about being angry at people, including your mother, and then you switched to talking about forgiving her. I think you retreated from your feelings.

P: Wow. Yeah, I see what you mean. It is just so hard to be angry, and I don't want to go around blaming everyone else for things that are really my responsibility.

A: You take your angry feelings and reverse them into self-hatred, and then you try and be really nice to the person you are angry with. But, inside I think you look down on them.

P: Well, I just feel more comfortable that way. The only person I don't do that with is my mother. I think that is because she will not go away. I am not afraid of her getting angry back or rejecting me and leaving me.

A: You are reluctant to be angry with men.

P: You're right, I can be pretty straightforward with women but I am afraid to be angry with men. I think they will leave me. Whenever I think of the word anger, immediately a giant picture pops up in my mind of my father. He was always so damn angry. He sits around the house all day drinking.

A: You sound angry and disgusted, almost superior.

P: I am disgusted with him, and I feel like he is a low life. At least my boyfriend has stopped drinking and is trying to get his act together. I do get angry with him. In the beginning of our relationship things were very different, but then the whole money thing started and it got bad. He is so dependent on me now, somehow I think I must like that. Except I feel dependent on him, too.

A: You do seem to want to control men. Perhaps when you

thought I just wanted your money last time, you were thinking along those lines, of me being dependent on you.

P: That is all true, but the real thing is I get really angry with
myself. I see all of these problems as my fault, no matter who
is involved. I can't be angry, except towards myself. That is
where the problem is, I am always feeling really angry with
myself. Even if I try to express my anger, it always comes
back to me. [*It "comes back" via projective identification.*]

A: I believe you take your anger at others and aim it at yourself
until you feel like a miserable victim, and then you feel like
you have a justified reason to be angry at the person who
seemed to put you there. It is a roundabout way of being
angry. [*I interpret her defence against the feelings of guilt and
loss.*]

P: I do that all the time. You have just hit on something I have
done for as long as I can remember. It makes me think of my
father. He always seemed so weak, and he would constantly
complain about all the things he felt were going wrong for
him and then he would get really angry. He had my mother
dependent on him, but he was always angry too.

A: You seem to control others with your victim role and then get
angry later.

P: But I don't want to put all the blame on these other people, I
orchestrate this stuff.

A: You're absolutely right.

P: I don't like therapy. It makes me think about everything that
I do. I never had to think before about what I did. Now
everywhere I look I am doing something. It is so tiring.

A: I wonder if the direct message is that you are angry with the
work you have to do here, but instead you make it sound like
you are a victim of this cruel process and then you can justi-
fiably be upset? [*I could have been more direct myself and said,
"You are angry with me but are scared I will seek revenge by
rejecting you."*]

P: I vaguely wondered that as the words were coming out of
my mouth.

Next session

P: I am going to go on my third job interview at that place I told you about, and I think that I have a pretty good chance of being hired. At the same time, I was told by a friend about this other place where her boyfriend works and I am going for an interview. It's a place that is always busy, and I know I would being making good money there. It also has a reputation for treating the employees really well. It's strange, though, because now I really don't want to leave where I am, I feel so attached to it. I have been there for a long time. I could do the job blindfolded.

A: Yet you often tell me about of how frustrated you are with the conditions.

P: Yes, I think I am afraid to get better; somehow I like the level I am at even though it goes nowhere.

A: You may be trying to be emotionally loyal to being the victim. That would prevent you from expressing your feelings of anger and your desires to assert yourself.

P: It was my boyfriend's birthday yesterday, and I met with him and gave him a card. Usually I would do a lot for him but I don't have any money right now. He didn't seem to care, he is like that. When my birthday came around last time, he didn't do much and I was really disappointed. All I wanted was for him to pay lots of attention to me throughout the day. You know, like kind of pamper me a little. But he didn't.

A: The sense I have is that you just hoped for it and when it didn't just appear you were very let down and felt victimized.

P: I think I see what you mean, like I could have taken some sort of action to get what I wanted, but instead I just sat around. I think I do that sometimes. I am afraid that that might happen when I go to this next interview, that they will get the impression that I don't care and then they won't give me the job.

A: It is almost like you feel you deserve things and it all should happen automatically. When it doesn't you are angry and disappointed. [*I am interpreting the demanding hunger she usually disguises with masochism.*]

P: That is the way it works. I tell myself that I was foolish to think that way and I don't deserve anything because I am such a loser. When I get angry I feel really guilty and that becomes the main thing on my mind.

A: So you find alternative ways of expressing it: being extra nice, or acting like a martyr.

P: I can certainly see how I learned that in my family. What comes to mind is how weak everyone was, all the time. It's disgusting. I want things to be different but I can't seem to do anything about it.

A: Your inaction leaves you feeling weak and furious.

P: Then I feel guilty and depressed.

A: Last time you were here you expressed your frustration and anger about therapy and how it wasn't going like you wanted. I wonder how you are dealing with that anger.

P: Well, that is different. This feels like a place that is safe, where I can express some of my feelings in a new way. Also, that was about the money I owed you and I was feeling really confused and guilty for not paying you.

A: So you became angry? [*She is angry that she has to give to me and it is easier to feel persecuted than to feel that she is hurting me.*]

P: Yeah, I was pretty confused, but then we worked it out.

Next session

P: Things are going pretty well; I feel up and confident. The interview with that one place went well, and I am going back. The other place also seems like a good deal, but I have to call them back. It all feels like it's coming together. It all sound so right. I was trying to remember what we talked about last time, regarding anger. It was important, but I can't seem to remember it. It was a breakthrough to me, about how I use anger or control, or something like that. I must be blocking.

A: What would be the reason to block an important break-through?

P: Well, so I don't have to look at it, so I can be in denial. Things can remain the same.

A: It is interesting that you block out something you feel is so important to you and then look to me to give it to you, like a teacher giving a lesson.

P: That is how I feel, like I need you to tell me what it was that was so important since I don't know any more.

A: Well, one of the items we discussed last time was how you gain control by being passive and how you can express your anger by becoming the victim. It seems that is what has happened here today.

P: I like to be in control, but I hate the idea of being a victim or being dependent on someone.

A: Yet you use one to get the other.

P: I hate the way it feels being the victim. I can't even stand the word. But I like being in control. I do see, when I think about it, how I am in control with my boyfriend. He will often ask me permission to do things, even simple things. I think of how he seems to play the role of someone who is being controlled. There is just something missing between us.

A: When you are controlling or when you're the victim, there is no way for you to have an equal and honest relationship.

P: I know I often feel like other people are doing things to me, like they are to blame. At the same time I never have felt comfortable with anger. I do blame a lot of people in my life. I blame my boyfriend for the whole money thing, I blame my boss for a lot of the crap that goes on at work, and I certainly blame myself for all sorts of things!

A: I wonder if blaming is a way that you can go with your feelings without ever having to take direct ownership of them.

P: What do you mean?

A: Well, a few times you have been frustrated with therapy. Instead of discussing these feelings with me, sharing them, and exploring them, you blame me for inflicting you with this nasty thing called therapy.

P: I see what you mean. You know, if I were really honest with myself I would end up leaving my boyfriend. I like the companionship and everything, but it really isn't what I want in the long run. There are things that he does that do make it all right. I guess there are things that make me feel like I should stay.

A: It sounds very flat the way you describe it.

P: I think I am just settling, that's what it is. I want him for what he can give me, which is companionship and attention. I need someone there, someone to call on the phone, someone to do stuff with, that sort of thing.

A: You are describing a friend or a buddy, but you don't include love and the other aspects of a romantic relationship.

P: Well, I would just leave him, but I can't imagine being alone. It feels like death. The companionship and the feeling of just having another person there is something I think I never experienced in my family. I need it really badly. That feeling of support or just knowing someone would answer if you called out. I don't think I ever had that. Ever since I started having a boyfriend, I have felt terrified of being alone. I just can't do it.

A: From all of your descriptions of your current relationship, I would say you are already quite alone in some ways.

P: You seem to want me to break up with him and that scares me.

A: Perhaps you are changing our relationship from one of sharing and discussing to one where I am to blame and I am causing you problems.

P: I see what you mean. I am just scared of being alone; it is worse than anything else I can imagine. I may be totally kidding myself. Actually, I am totally kidding myself about my boyfriend and how close we are, but I need him. I also need the phone calls from my ex-boyfriend; they keep me going. Without them, I would be so lonely.

A: Yet you have stated that if you were honest with yourself you "wouldn't give him the fucking time of day".

P: That's right! I am just desperate. The fear of being alone is really overwhelming and I just can't get over it. I know I use work as a decoy that way. I work all the time, and especially at night, so I don't have to ever be alone. The idea of being alone at night is especially frightening. I guess I would rather put up with all this controlling and victim stuff than to risk being alone.

A: The sad paradox is that by being controlling or passive you end up very alone. I hope you can tell me more about how scary it is to be alone. [*It was very moving how she was able to reveal so much of her fear of losing her object and being alone in a way that felt like annihilation.*]

Next session

I received a phone message from Veronica. She was frantic and distressed. She told me that for some reason her insurance company had denied her any reimbursement for her therapy. She felt that this added a factor to her already marginal financial situation that "put her over the edge". She told me she had to take a break and regroup herself and her finances and hoped that I understood "what pressure she was under".

I called her and suggested that we could continue therapy but with a reduction in the fee to something she could manage. I also suggested we look into the insurance problem. She cited her desire to continue therapy, her fear of the guilt that a reduction in fee would bring, and her continued wish to "take a break until things got better". She again mentioned that I might not appreciate the type of intense pressure and stress she felt herself to be under. I said that she may be under pressure from the feelings she revealed in the last session. She said, "Yes, but it is a money issue." She ended by saying, "I hope you will take me back in a month or so, thank you." She never called back. After a month or two, I called her and she told me she was almost homeless and couldn't afford therapy, let alone a place to live, because of having to pay all her boyfriend's bills.

This was a difficult patient who was an expert at keeping herself enraged, miserable, and persecuted while toiling on behalf of her needy objects. She continually projected her life-sustaining desires and urges to receive emotional nutrition into her objects, leaving her to deal with the darker, hopeless side of herself. Betty Joseph (1982) states: "it is, however, important also to consider where the pull toward life and sanity is. I believe that this part of the patient is located in the analyst, which in part, accounts for the patient's apparent extreme passivity and indifference in progress" (p. 449).

The patient I presented was constantly projecting her drive towards life into me and others. She felt like giving up, and I stood in for her desire to sort things out and progress. This splitting and projection leads to a tug-of-war in which the analyst often is pushing the patient to work harder and have a better attitude. Therefore, it is not only the life force that is projected into the object, but the sadistic aspects of the ego as well. The pushy, controlling parts of the patient return, via projective identification, through the analyst's acting out of a lecturing parent.

With such masochistic paranoid–schizoid patients, there is a link between loss, the projection of life forces, and destructive narcissism. The patient's ego feels abandoned and lost, wanting love and protection. This is the result of splitting, projective identification, and re-internalization of hostile and demanding oral and anal phantasies. Anticipating the object being hurt and overwhelmed and subsequently vengeful, the ego employs destructive narcissistic defences. The feeling of "I need help" shifts to "you need help" to "I am being pursued by this pathetic parasite". However, the ego needs its object for security and survival, so it must suffer and be a prisoner to a weak, clinging object. This leads to further paranoia, a feeling of "I can't escape this parasite!" So, via projective identification, splitting, and envy, the ego discharges its craving, only to have it boomerang back with a vengeance.

"Lucy"

This is the case of a disturbed, masochistic woman who focused on tragedy and bodily problems as a way of coping with her internal objects and her overwhelming anger and anxiety. She maintained somatic delusions and dramatic phantasies as a way to attack and defend her internal objects that she felt threatened by and felt the need to protect. Her emphasis on her body created uncomfortable countertransference feelings in me. This was the result of her projective-identification efforts to bring us into specific, narrow, and repetitious ways of being with each other.

In treating Lucy, I became more aware of the link between masochism and the struggles of the paranoid–schizoid position. In her case, this was framed around the fixed phantasy of somatic distress and external tragedy. Her somatic focus was a form of acting out which kept our relationship concrete and distant. This protected her from me and me from her but also left her alone and frustrated. Lucy's somatic, masochistic cage left her terribly envious of my ability to function independently and furious of her own hunger for dependence.

Lucy, a 50-year-old woman, came to see me on the advice of her boyfriend, for "general purposes". With this vague introduction, I began meeting with her twice a week. We left the option open to increase the frequency to three or four times a week, and this happened after six months. After the initial consultation, I was left with a feeling of being with someone who would rapidly show me a one side of herself while hiding other aspects of herself.

During the first session, I noticed that Lucy presented herself as a lifelong victim and kept bringing up stories of bad physical health and various tragedies. Also, I felt distant from her. As she told me about herself, I felt strangely uninterested. I wondered if I was trying to protect myself from something or if she had projected certain cold and dismissive parts of herself into me. I also wondered if this was a signal about how unreachable she was and how hard it would be to make contact with her during the upcoming months.

Lucy told me she had been an unwanted baby. Child-protection services had removed her several times from her mother's home. Her mother had turned her over to an adoption agency when Lucy was 3 years old. She was adopted by a couple who had no children of their own. Lucy's father was an abusive and controlling man. He put her down, telling her that it had been a mistake to adopt her and that she should be grateful to have a home. He was very cruel physically, burning her and hitting her. During Lucy's adolescence, he called her a whore and a useless, selfish person.

Since both parents had worked full time, Lucy had lived with an uncle until she was 8, when the uncle died. Lucy recalls her uncle as a loving person who stood up for her and always reassured her that everything would be ok. When Lucy talked about this special relationship, I felt that she was more real and accessible to me, even though the strange disjointedness remained.

As Lucy told me about her early years in elementary school and high school, I noticed a pattern. Each story started out relatively positive but would take a bad turn. Her love of science was suddenly soured by several classmates who beat her. Her love of sports was ruined when her father ignored her track and field meet. At these times, I felt strangely off balance, as though she had involved me in a bait-and-switch con game. I had trusted her and now felt duped.

Lucy lived with her parents from when she was 9 years old until she was 30. Her relationship with her family remained unchanged during these years. Instead of gradually separating from her family and feeling more autonomous, she remained a persecuted child. She told me of many dismal and abusive relationships with men, including two failed marriages. The few men she felt fond of, who treated her tenderly, all died by some tragic means. I wondered where I stood.

In her thirties, Lucy had several miscarriages. These tragic events were related in a way that again left me suspicious and unusually unattuned. Similarly, I felt distant when she told me of her numerous suicide attempts. All in all, my countertransference was a combination of "I don't believe you" and "I don't care".

Lucy had a limited health-insurance plan and a low-paying job. Therefore, we worked out a fee that was based on her ability to pay. In negotiating her fee, I thought to myself of how her funds would run out in several months and we might have to end the treatment. I then thought of how I didn't picture her as capable of being more successful in her job and paying more in the upcoming months. She had said that all her relationships fell apart at some point, so I imagined that this might be one of many ways that could happen. Here, I felt our alliance would slowly collapse, leaving one of us bad or hopeless.

Session 2

At the start of her second session, Lucy got up from her waiting-room chair and coins fell out of her pockets onto the floor. She looked at them but walked on into my office. I asked about it, and she said the coins were unimportant, "only pennies". I commented that she was afraid that she had to pick between being available to me or being available to herself and that she feared I would be angry if she tended to her own value. She said, "Maybe, I hadn't thought of it that way."

Then she showed me her hand. She had a Band-Aid on one finger. Lucy said she had broken her fingers in a fight with her boyfriend. She said that the doctor told her not to use it for six weeks. I was flushed with a feeling of disbelief, like I was witnessing a con job and one that was not done well. I felt pulled in to be a certain way with her. I felt forced to pretend that I cared. She went on to tell me what a bastard the nurse was. The rest of the hour was spent with her telling me about how violent her boyfriends and family have always been over the years.

Lucy also told me that she had come down with a violent case of the flu that left her "physically devastated". She told me about being unable to move, not able to get out of bed, her throat raw from coughing all night and all day, being unable to sleep or eat for days, and how she had "thrown up her guts for days". She told me she ached so much she was sure she was dying.

It seemed that she used projective identification to communicate, but mostly to discharge various aspects of her internal experience. She put an incredulous, uncaring father part of herself into me and related to that part as a neglected, abused orphan who was always in pain. At other times, she projected a trapped, helpless, and frustrated little girl into me and related to that part as a dominating father. These intrapsychic dynamics were instigated and maintained by her masochistic interpersonal style and her hysterical, somatic focus. While I initially tried to interpret these interactions, what worked best was to contain them and silently interpret them as a test of trust and endurance in our relationship. Lucy's somatic and masochistic way of relating to me slowly decreased over the first year of therapy.

What was harder to understand and more difficult to intervene with was how she used all these ways of relating to build up a false sense of closeness which was then abruptly torn down. She seemed only vaguely aware of her participation in this process and very resistant to exploring it. My sense was that she didn't want to give up her favourite weapon and also felt terrified about the idea of not having that weapon to focus her life around.

Session 3

At the start of the session she went to the analytic couch, sat on it, and showed me the paperback she had been reading.

A: Something is getting in the way of you lying down.

P: My neck really hurts, so if I lie down it will get worse. I pinched a nerve in my neck a while ago and I could hardly move. I thought I would be in a wheelchair. There was a shooting pain that went into my head, and I have never felt that kind of pain before. I thought I was dying. Now, I can't move my head all the way in any direction. I probably need physical therapy or a chiropractor. Also, I need to see your face. I feel you want me to fall backwards and you are saying you will catch me, but I don't trust you. I have to see your face to know if I can trust you.

A: Let's try to understand why you don't trust me and how you think I will just let you fall.

P: I can't believe my boyfriend really loves me. I guess people always have left me, and I still expect that and wait and see and then say, "See, I knew it!"

A: It's like you want to prove that I will abandon you?

P: Maybe. I still want my father's love and acceptance, but I can't get it. And everyone dies. My special friend Joe, he died in a drug shoot-out, and then my aunt died too. Joe was so special, he knew how to manage me and calm me down. When I got raped, I stayed with him. He let me just be me. [*I thought she was instructing me on how to be with her as well.*]

A: It's very important that he accepted you as you were.

P: Yes. He told me it was ok, no matter what. He taught me how to fish too.

A: I wonder if he treated you like you wished your father would have, caring and accepting.

P: I guess so. I don't know, though. We never had sex. I didn't want to, because I thought it might change things.

A: It's interesting how you are mentioning not having sex right after my comment about your father. Was there sexual tension between you and your father?

P: No, but he would always barge in on me when I was dressing and when I was sleeping. I was 29 years old. I didn't need that kind of shit. Anyway, Joe was a good man.

A: Maybe you are hoping to trust me but you're worried if I will be accepting and caring or barge in on your feelings and thoughts.

P: I always get rid of people before they have a chance to hurt me. I trust my friend Sam a lot, but I never want to lean on him, 'cause I don't want to burn him out. I am always seen as the one who is fucked up and needing help. I want to get his help, but I worry that I will drain him and burn him out. When I fell down the stairs last year, I broke my leg and had to get a steel plate in it. It hurt so bad I couldn't believe it. It was swollen up for weeks, and I had to take pain medicine to just survive. It still hurts at certain times. [*She tells me the gory details of the accident.*] Sam helped me out, but I felt like I was a burden.

A: Maybe you're worried you will drain me and make me uninterested?

P: I feel I am opening up to you, and I don't know if I should. What if you are overwhelmed with all that is inside me. I

want to have faith in you and I am opening up, but I don't
know if it is safe to do that because I don't know you yet.
Maybe I am trusting you too soon, maybe I should hold back.

A: A bit like with your boyfriend.

P: Yes, and with my old boyfriends too. How can I trust his love
when he gets so violent, breaking shit and yelling? He is
always causing trouble and something gets broken. We don't
have any dishes left 'cause of that. [*She tells me stories of
various violent fights she has been in and all the destruction that
happens.*]

A: How are you two getting along right now?

P: It's fine lately because we don't talk to each other. Although,
I snuggled with him today in the morning but then I left
really quick. It was too much of a good thing. I don't want to
ruin it. [*I feel she is worried that she causes her objects to suffer,
because of her neediness and then they retaliate.*]

A: What do you mean?

P: If he woke up, he might want to have sex. I don't want that
right now. After he started breaking shit I stopped wanting
to have sex. He is always pissed off and it scares me, so I
turned off. I care about him a lot, but I want the fighting to
stop. He blames me. I do get shitty and yell too, but I try not
to. I don't like it. I don't like hurting people with words. I
hope that if I treat them nice they will treat me nice. I have
such a horrible headache from the fighting that I can barely
see. I have been taking so much aspirin that I have ulcers. I
wake up with a splitting headache and it doesn't go away
until I go to sleep. It hurts so bad I can hardly concentrate at
work. [*She tells me a story of how she feels overburdened by her job
as well.*]

I am thinking that her attempts to be nice to people and not
hurt them are not genuine but are based on trying to prevent a
horrible battle, a loss, and pain; she therefore tries to find a way
to pacify her objects.

A: You seem excited to show me your book. Is that something
you are into yourself?

P: No, my true love is music. In school I played the harp and the drums. I really loved it. But, after four kids tried to rape me I gave it up. I ran away and ended up falling down and splitting my skull open. I had to get stitched up, and I lost a lot of blood. I had to stay in the hospital overnight because they thought I might have a concussion or something. I was scared to go out of the house for months. Also, my father said "big fucking deal", so I threw my music prize away. He said I was the daughter of a whore. If I ever held hands with a guy or kissed him goodnight, my father yelled at me for being a whore. I took modern dance in high school and really liked it, but my first husband told me I danced like a slut. I was a stripper at one point, I think I did it to spite my father. It was a real rush. My boyfriend managed a strip club but he left me for another stripper. He is dead now, kidney failure.

A: So you get close to what you want, and then it ends in tragedy.

P: Yes. I cried so much for him. I really admired him.

A: I wonder if you are so happy to be close to a person that somehow you don't notice other parts of them that later turn out to be hurtful.

P: Could be. With my second husband I only knew him three months before we got married and that was mostly on the phone. He asked me to trust him and give him a chance and then he kicked me in the teeth. Actually, he pulled my hair out and hit me in the back with his fist so my kidneys were sore for weeks. I had a problem going to the bathroom for a while. I still have terrible back pain from that.

A: You were telling me how horrible your boyfriend is last time I saw you, but today you seem to feel better about him.

P: Well, I still want to move out and be on my own but I do still like him, so I don't know. He keeps threatening to kick me out.

A: Our time is over for tonight. I will see you next time.

P: Ok. Boy, my neck sure hurts. I have had problems with my back for a long time. Both my neck and back are really sore a lot of times. At times, the pain gets so severe that I can't

concentrate on anything and I have to go to bed. But I can't
sleep because I am so uncomfortable.

I think of how at the start of the session she tried to bond with
me with the book and now how she is trying to bond with me
through her body complaints. She seems to be fishing around
to find a way to be with me that will endear herself to me, but
also a way she can control me with servitude.

A: Maybe, it hurts to leave, after you start trusting me.

P: No. I just have this terrible ache. Some days are worse than
others. Some days my whole body hurts so much that I don't
want to even leave the house.

Session 4

P: Boy, there are a lot of idiots on the road. Ok, what do you
want to know?

A: Whatever is on your mind. [*Here, I miss how she puts me in the
role of interrogator.*]

P: I had a chance to talk with my friend Sally; that was good.
She said she would tell my father to stop telling me that I'm
adopted and should be grateful. I wish she lived closer. She
said I could live with her if I ever needed to.

A: She looks after you.

P: Yes. She would babysit me when I was little. She would get
me special toys. She was always happy to have me around. I
always wished she was my mother. One time she spanked
me for running into the street. I really made her feel bad for
that, and she ended up getting me ice-cream to get me to stop
crying. She never told my father. It was our little secret. I was
so sad when she left. I got really sick. She had to reassure me
that I could always call her.

A: It's the one relationship you have told me about that you
don't feel is contaminated or has turned bad. [*Actually, I think
it did feel bad. It was a terrible loss. However, it didn't seem to
lodge into her mind and body as an attacking and annihilating
experience that took her mind over.*]

P: I never told people about the rape until two years ago, but when I had a miscarriage it reminded me of it and I felt to blame for the abortion. I told Sally and I was worried I would lose her respect. My father would have really blamed me for that.

A: In telling me about it, you want my respect and acceptance. I think that is on your mind a great deal.

P: Maybe. I don't know. It's nice to know Sally admires me and supports me, sometimes I feel really shaky and, like, I won't make it. [*I think she felt scared by my pointing to her dependence and hunger, so she dismissed me in favour of the object that she safely controls.*]

A: How so?

P: I feel like the world would be better off without me. I have never contributed anything or accomplished anything. Sally has her own business. I always give up on things. I never follow through. I kind of like my job right now, but it's not what I really want.

A: Maybe you hold yourself back in some way.

P: I used to be a good dance teacher at the community centre, but I'm too old for that now. I have started to have arthritis in my legs an arms. [*She tells me lengthy details about her joint pains.*] I am very creative with crafts. I sew a lot, but I never finish any of my projects.

A: Perhaps your anger gets in the way. [*I am thinking that she is so angry at her objects that she refuses to give to them. She wishes to control them by making them take care of her, in loving and hating ways. Another path I could have followed would be about her feelings of competition with Sally and her envy of what she has.*]

P: I never thought of it that way before. I think my energy level is so low. There is never enough time for what I want to do. It's always a big rush. I feel so frustrated. Always tired. Often, I feel nauseous and dizzy. [*She goes into the details.*] This weekend was all right. We went to the museum. I fed the pigeons, but they all attacked me and pecked at my shoes. It was fun and kind of creepy at the same time. I like simple things, blowing bubbles in the air.

A: You're dissatisfied with your life? [*I choose to go with this general question rather than address the specific image of her being attacked and overwhelmed from inside. With these types of patients, one often has to start at the point of greatest externalization and work back.*]

P: Well, I wish I was better at what I do. I'd like to get a Master degree in music, take some music classes.

A: What stops you?

P: Money and timing with my job. I'd like to go scuba-diving again too. It's so peaceful down there; I had always wanted to do that and I finally did. The first time was horrible, I almost burst an eardrum, but the second time was better. The ache and pain was terrible. Blood was pouring out of both ears and I was crying and couldn't stop screaming. My mother thought I should have quit; she said, "You are a glutton for punishment." I just wasn't prepared. So I felt really positive about it when I did. I did get slammed into some rocks when I came up. I was black and blue for weeks. I had thirty pounds of heavy equipment on my back. It was so heavy I thought I wouldn't be able to move. I was sore for weeks later. I was all torn up from the rocks too. I had gashes all up and down my legs. They didn't heal for a long time. [*She tells me the details.*]

A: You seem to use pain as a way to relate to me.

P: I guess so. All my boyfriends have been pretty bad. They all promised to be nice and then ended up punching me out, pointing guns at me, yelling at me. My girlfriend told me what you just said too. The one nice guy I had wasn't around long enough for me to learn different. My girlfriend told me that I have the right to my own thoughts and feelings. I am at a point in my life where I want it all to work. Maybe I try too hard.

A: What do you mean?

P: I stay too long in the relationship. I could be alone, but I want to be with someone, to share things. My boyfriend judges me for just about everything. He wants me to do things his way. He calls me stupid. He likes heavy-metal music and I like rap music.

A: It's amazing how you would be together, given these differences. [*I go with her dramatic view as a means to meet her half-way.*]

P: Yes, it is. He says he is crazy about me. He can be caring, he makes me breakfast sometimes even though it's not what I want to eat. My father used to give me shit for not eating breakfast. He used to like to punish me publicly, so everyone would know I was a bad kid.

A: It sounds so cruel. You bring it up right after telling me about getting breakfast made for you. Maybe its uncomfortable to be loved, you feel guilty. [*I think she is feeling guilty for draining him, so she tries to erase what she took.*]

P: I had to obey and mind. There was never any room for mistakes. I had to be seen and not heard.

A: I suspect you put yourself down now, like he did.

P: I never give myself credit for anything. I just do it but I never see it as something to get credit for. I do get motivated. I made all these party favours and a lot of my friends bought them for New Year's. To me it was no big deal, just something I like. [*Here again, I feel strange. She sounds like a child who made some money off a Kool-Aid stand.*]

A: It is hard for you to get excited about yourself. [*I use my countertransference to inform my interpretation.*]

P: Yes. In my twenties, I felt that all my girlfriends were so beautiful and I was so plain. I was so envious of them. But they always admired me. I never understood that. They told me I was very pretty, but I never get compliments at home or from my husband. If I get a compliment, I'm embarrassed.

A: I wonder if that all makes it hard to share yourself with me.

---

*In the United States, some children earn pocket-money by selling Kool-Aid, a soft-drink, to passers-by.

P: Yes it does. I don't know what you want. I can't tell.

A: So just telling me what comes to your mind is hard because you are trying to figure out what to give to me.

P: I think to myself, "Why would he care?" I'm sorry, I don't mean to be rude.

A: I think you are challenging me to care, but you are scared that I might not.

P: Well, thank you for telling me that. I often don't know if I am being rude. I get defensive.

A: If I seem to care for you, you get uptight to protect yourself.

At the beginning of the treatment, Lucy mostly related to me with horrific tales of disaster and physical ailments. My counter-transference was often irritation and disbelief. As I tried to interpret her projective-identification process with me and how she gave me a dose of her own loss, betrayal, and persecution, this shifted a bit. Lucy slowly gave up some of her masochistic methods of assaulting me and provoking me and shifted to playful teasing. She would tease me about my manner of speech or dress and also make seductive and flirty moves towards me.

As she shifted from her somatic, masochistic stance to a flirting little girl who picked on me, she also revealed various "secrets". She told me that she had the ability to "fly" whenever she wanted to. She described a disassociation process whereby she would fly around the room and above buildings, watching herself and everyone going about their business.

Lucy also revealed several childhood memories of being brutally punished and abused by her father. When she told me about her traumatic past and her "flying ability", I noticed that we seemed to be connected in a much more real way. When she told me of being burned, starved, and prevented from using the bathroom, I felt agony and tremendous sadness for her. While she was still distant and defended, she was able to be more vulnerable with me and it impacted me rather than leaving me hollow. This new trust was mysterious. It was genuine while it lasted, yet it still was a set-up that gave way to a more negative and thorny way of being with me.

She usually spent her hours discussing various details of what went on at work, or the ups and downs of her relationship to her boyfriend. Every once in a while, she would begin to tell me a little bit about her feelings of being abandoned by her mother and how she worried she had been so unlovable that no one could have tolerated her. These quick, darting excursions into a much more real place inside herself were mostly initiated by my transference comments. Such a comment would initially stop her cold. Lucy would fall silent and then change the subject. Then she would come back to it and make an association to the traumatic feelings that she usually tried to ignore. So, transference interpretations helped her make associations to genetic material, which defended against exploration of the transference. It was her compromise.

Throughout her treatment, now in its third year, Lucy missed many sessions because of what she said were the rigorous demands of her job. Part of these dynamics were her wanting revenge on me as her controlling father. However, what I choose to emphasize through interpretations was the way that she both strove to prove her love and loyalty to her boss while managing to get me to experience the frustration and confusion of loss that she had felt growing up. She was able to take these interpretations in only gradually, in bits and pieces. It is still unclear if the treatment will collapse altogether or will manage to continue. The balance of trust and growth versus loss and rejection still looms in the transference.

A massive projective-identification process seems to be the principle force shaping Lucy's transference. The table has been turned, and I am left to experience her own agony with loss and persecution. Over and over again, I begin to trust her and feel deeply sympathetic for a person who has suffered so gravely in life. Just as I feel connected with this brave soul, she breaks the connection and turns into a cruel and distant stranger. I feel manipulated, duped, and betrayed.

Lucy's transference and projective-identification manoeuvres were a vicious cycle in which she (intrapsychically and interpersonally) acted like the wounded bird who sacrifices herself as a decoy in order to draw attention away from the nest. In Lucy's case, she assaulted me with tales of physical pain and tragedy as a way of diverting my attention from her unconscious fears and wishes. These involved both loving and aggressive motives. She hoped to avoid the revenge of her objects she felt she had destroyed. It was her way of saying, "Please spare me, I am already so injured and punished, please don't kill me." It was also a masochistic way of becoming close and intimate with me and placing me in a dominant position. Finally, her somatic focus and masochistic stance served, through projective identification, continually to destroy the object out of rage and revenge for the pain she suffered. Her somatic vehicle was far safer and more defensible than a more direct approach to her external and internal objects.

Summary and conclusions

I have proposed that loss within the paranoid–schizoid position is under-represented in the literature. Therefore, I have outlined the process of loss as organized in this early developmental experience. Melanie Klein and a few of her followers, mainly Hanna Segal, have discussed the fear of losing the idealized object and the corresponding fear of bad objects. In agreement, I find that patients in the paranoid–schizoid position usually have a rather fragile hold on an idealized, intrapsychic object that they crave union with, for safety and emotional nutrition. The ego's projections of aggression and envy easily disrupt this closeness. External trauma is often an additional factor. For a variety of reasons, both intrapsychic and interpersonal, this hoped-for and much-desired union can be broken. At that point, the good part-objects turn into attacking bad part-objects. This is the nature of loss in the paranoid–schizoid position. It is not a depressive fear of hurting the object. It is a combination of losing unity with an object that is felt to be necessary for survival and a shift of helpful, loving objects turning into persecutory bad objects.

Through PI and splitting, loving aspects of the self are projected into the object and the ego tries to attach itself to that now loving and loved object. Due to various internal (excessive aggression, greed, envy, and fear) and external (a mother who is unavailable emotionally for some reason and/or an environmental trauma) difficulties, the desired object and the desired state of union with that object are not available. The ego feels as though what it needs for survival has been taken away, is unavailable, broken. The angry, chaotic, and scary feelings that follow are projected into the object, creating a shift from a wonderful feeding mother-object to an angry attacking bad object. Because the object is not entirely separate from the ego in the paranoid–schizoid position, this feels like a threat of annihilation. Excessive PI creates ego–object de-differentiation. Therefore, the loss of the object is equal to the loss of the self.

In normal development, projective identification fosters a beneficial cycle of creating stable, containing, and loving objects that help build stable, containing, and loving internal ego and superego structure. This in turn fosters the creation of hope, creativity, and care for others. When loss is a central factor in the development of the infantile ego, PI comes to bear in a way that is destructive and fosters a cycle of persecutory anxiety. More and more bad objects are created through the projection of anger and turmoil. These objects are felt to deny the ego any level of attachment, love, or feeding. This generates more rage and envy. Loss and PI begin to fracture and fragment the early ego, causing even more reliance on destructive forms of PI and splitting.

Symbol formation is also an aspect of early development that hopefully builds within a cycle of healthy PI and mitigates unbearable loss. By projecting internal conflicts and object-related concerns onto various ideas and activities, creativity and sublimation offer relief from paranoid–schizoid or depressive anxieties. However, if the world feels hostile and abandonment is an ongoing threat (internally or externally), the ego is prone to excessive PI. The ego needs good internal and external objects plus overall sufficient ego strength to transform paranoid–schizoid and depressive anxieties into symbols. This is especially so in the paranoid–schizoid position, where ego–object differentiation is not complete. Separation, in a healthy sense, is necessary for optimal symbol function. In contrast, loss leaves the ego surrounded by persecutory objects and symbol equation, where internal and external reality become the same.

Loss within the paranoid–schizoid position and its relationship to PI remain areas in need of more exploration. Some work has been done theoretically. In addition to more conceptualization, work also needs to occur with analytic technique. It is still unclear how best to proceed technically with patients using PI to deal with loss in the paranoid–schizoid position. Modern Kleinians have not thought out as amply as they might what to do and what to say.

It seems important that the immediate, dual anxieties be addressed interpretatively and in the transference. These would be, in the first place, the phantasy of being separated from or abandoned by the ideal object, who is necessary for basic survival as well as for love, support, and nourishment. At this point, the favoured good object turns into an angry, attacking bad object ready to hunt the ego down. In treatment, one of these feelings is often used to defend against the other. However, the working-through process would require the exploration of both. PI remains the vehicle of these primitive anxieties. Therefore, interpretative efforts need to focus on the mechanism of PI as it occurs in the transference.

The emergence of greater symbolic function is a signal of progress. Gradual retraction of both good and bad projections from the object signals the process of separation and contact with the reality principle. This in turn brings entry into the depressive position where loss takes on a different meaning and reparation, creativity, and sublimation can take over to heal some of the grief.

Optimally, paranoid–schizoid loss shifts into depressive mourning. The ego gradually gives up its demanding quest for the original ideal object and moves into a more reality-based relationship to the world. The remaining incompleteness and singular yearning for a perfect union with an all-gratifying breast turns into a more inclusive sublimation and symbolization process that brings the ego into a mutuality with its objects and the external world. What was lost is not ever found or recovered, but is re-discovered in new, ever-changing forms.

REFERENCES

Bion, W. (1959). Attacks on linking. *International Journal of Psycho-Analysis, 30*: 308–315.

Bion, W. (1962). A theory of thinking. *International Journal of Psycho-Analysis, 33*: 306–310.

Caper, R. (1988). *Immaterial Facts: Freud's Discovery of Psychic Reality and Klein's Development of His Work.* New York: Jason Aronson.

Carstairs, K. (1992). Paranoid–schizoid or symbiotic? *International Journal of Psycho-Analysis, 73*: 71–85.

Feldman, M. (1997). Splitting and projective identification. In: *The Contemporary Kleinians of London*, edited by R. Schafer. Madison, CT: International Universities Press.

Freud, S. (1916). Some character-types met with in psycho-analytic work: the "exceptions". *S.E., 14*, pp. 311–315.

Grotstein, J. (1986). *Splitting and Projective Identification.* New York: Jason Aronson.

Hinshelwood, R. D. (1991). *A Dictionary of Kleinian Thought.* London: Free Association Books.

Hurvich, M. (1998). The influence of object relations theory on contemporary freudian technique. In: *The Modern Freudians*, edited by

C. Ellman, S. Grand, M. Silvan, & S. Ellman. Northvale, NJ: Jason Aronson.

Joseph, B. (1959). An aspect of the repetition compulsion. *International Journal of Psycho-Analysis, 40*: 213.

Joseph, B. (1982). Addiction to near-death. *International Journal of Psycho-Analysis, 63*: 449–456.

Joseph, B. (1985). Transference: the total situation. *International Journal of Psycho-Analysis, 66*: 447.

Klein, M. (1935). A contribution to the psychogenesis of manic-depressive states. *The Writings of Melanie Klein, Vol. I*. London: Hogarth Press, 1975 [reprinted London: Karnac Books, 1992].

Klein, M. (1936). Weaning. *The Writings of Melanie Klein, Vol. I*. London: Hogarth Press, 1975 [reprinted London: Karnac Books, 1992].

Klein, M. (1937). Love, guilt and reparation. *The Writings of Melanie Klein, Vol. I*. London: Hogarth Press, 1975 [reprinted London: Karnac Books, 1992].

Klein, M. (1940). Mourning and its relation to manic-depressive states. *The Writings of Melanie Klein, Vol. I*. London: Hogarth Press, 1975 [reprinted London: Karnac Books, 1992].

Klein, M. (1946). Notes on some schizoid mechanisms. *The Writings of Melanie Klein, Vol. III*. London: Hogarth Press, 1975 [reprinted London: Karnac Books, 1993].

Klein, M. (1948). On the theory of anxiety and guilt. *The Writings of Melanie Klein, Vol. III*. London: Hogarth Press, 1975 [reprinted London: Karnac Books, 1993].

Klein, M. (1950). On the criteria for the termination of a psychoanalysis. *The Writings of Melanie Klein, Vol. III*. London: Hogarth Press, 1975 [reprinted London: Karnac Books, 1993].

Klein, M. (1952a). The mutual influences in the development of ego and id. *The Writings of Melanie Klein, Vol. III*. London: Hogarth Press, 1975 [reprinted London: Karnac Books, 1993].

Klein, M. (1952b). On observing the behaviour of young infants. *The Writings of Melanie Klein, Vol. III*. London: Hogarth Press, 1975 [reprinted London: Karnac Books, 1993].

Klein, M. (1952c). Some theoretical conclusions regarding the emotional life of the infant. *The Writings of Melanie Klein, Vol. III*. London: Hogarth Press, 1975 [reprinted London: Karnac Books, 1993].

REFERENCES   195

Klein, M. (1955). On identification. *The Writings of Melanie Klein, Vol. III.* London: Hogarth Press, 1975 [reprinted London: Karnac Books, 1993].

Klein, M. (1957). Envy and gratitude. *The Writings of Melanie Klein, Vol. III.* London: Hogarth Press, 1975 [reprinted London: Karnac Books, 1993].

Klein, M. (1959). Our adult world and its roots in infancy. *The Writings of Melanie Klein, Vol. III.* London: Hogarth Press, 1975 [reprinted London: Karnac Books, 1993].

Klein, M. (1963). On the sense of loneliness. *The Writings of Melanie Klein, Vol. III.* London: Hogarth Press, 1975 [reprinted London: Karnac Books, 1993].

Likierman, M. (1993). Primitive object love in Melanie Klein's thinking: early theoretical influences. *International Journal of Psycho-Analysis, 74:* 241–253.

Mitchell, S. (1981). The origin and nature of the "object" in the theories of Klein and Fairbairn. *Contemporary Psychoanalysis, 17:* 374–398.

Moore, B., & Fine, B. (1990). *Psychoanalytic Terms and Concepts.* New Haven, CT: Yale University Press.

Ogden, T. (1984). Instinct, phantasy, and psychological deep structure—a reinterpretation of aspects of the work of Melanie Klein. *Contemporary Psychoanalysis, 20:* 500–525.

Perlow, M. (1995). *Understanding Mental Objects.* New York: Routledge.

Quinodoz, J.-M. (1983). *The Taming of Solitude: Separation Anxiety in Psychoanalysis.* New York: Routledge.

Riesenberg-Malcolm, R. (1997). Conceptualization of clinical facts. In: *The Contemporary Kleinians of London,* edited by R. Schafer. Madison, CT: International Universities Press.

Rosenfeld, H. (1964). On the psychopathology of narcissism. *International Journal of Psycho-Analysis, 45:* 332–337.

Rosenfeld, H. (1983). Primitive object relations and mechanisms. *International Journal of Psycho-Analysis, 64:* 261–267.

Rosenfeld, H. (1988). On masochism: a theoretical and clinical approach. In: *Masochism: Current Psychoanalytic Perspectives,* edited by R. Glick & D. Meyers. New York: Analytic Press.

Schafer, R. (Ed.) (1997). *The Contemporary Kleinians of London.* Madison, CT: International Universities Press.

Segal, H. (1957). Notes on symbol formation. *International Journal of Psycho-Analysis, 38*: 39–45.

Segal, H. (1969). "Discussion." British Psychoanalytical Society Symposium on Envy and Jealousy.

Segal, H. (1974). *An Introduction to the Work of Melanie Klein.* New York: Basic Books.

Segal, H. (1981). *The Work of Hanna Segal: A Kleinian Approach to Clinical Practice.* New York: Jason Aronson.

Segal, H. (1983). Some implications of Melanie Klein's work. *International Journal of Psycho-Analysis, 64*: 269–276.

Segal, H. (1997a). Manic reparation. In: *The Contemporary Kleinians of London,* edited by R. Schafer. Madison, CT: International Universities Press.

Segal, H. (1997b). Phantasy and reality. In: *The Contemporary Kleinians of London,* edited by R. Schafer. Madison, CT: International Universities Press.

Segal, H. (1997c). *Psychoanalysis, Literature, and War: Papers 1972–1995,* edited by John Steiner. London: Routledge.

Spillius, E. B. (1992). Clinical experiences of projective identification. In: *Clinical Lectures on Klein and Bion,* edited by Robin Anderson. London: Routledge.

Spillius, E. B. (1994). Developments in Kleinian thought: overview and personal view. *Psychoanalytic Inquiry, 14* (3): 324–364.

Spillius, E. B. (1997). Varieties of envious experience. In: *The Contemporary Kleinians of London,* edited by R. Schafer. Madison, CT: International Universities Press.

St. Clair, M. (1986). *Object Relations and Self Psychology: An Introduction.* Monterey, CA: Brooks/Cole.

Steiner, J. (1997). The interplay between pathological organizations and the paranoid–schizoid and depressive positions. In: *The Contemporary Kleinians of London,* edited by R. Schafer. Madison, CT: International Universities Press.

Weininger, O., & Harris, R. (1983). On primary masochism. *Journal of the Melanie Klein Society, 1* (2): 53–60.

INDEX

abandonment, fear of:
  loss of good object, 31
  by objects [clinical example], 58–60
  see also loss; persecutory anxieties;
      separation
absence:
  experienced as persecution, 20, 27,
      28
  as fear of loss of good object, 31
  see also loss; separation
affect, difficulty of interpretations
      with paranoid–schizoid
      patients, 121
aggression, 189
  and deprivation, 100
  displaced by symbol formation, 34
  oral, 102, 156
anal impulses:
  and oral, 9–10
  -sadistic, 3
analytic relationship, 116–118
  guilt and projective identification,
      111
  projections, 116
  see also countertransference;
      transference

anger:
  countertransference, 153
  victim [clinical example], 165–170
annihilation:
  fear of, 20–21, 25, 26, 27, 152
  paranoid–schizoid loss, 102
  symbol equation, 33
  use of masochism, 115
anxiety(ies), 2
  defensive function of the ego, 6
  depressive anxieties, 21, 22, 25, 28,
      29, 30
  loss, 25–26
  neurotic, 25
  objective anxiety, 25
  paranoid–schizoid position, 4
  phantasies, 8, 15
  schizoid, 100
  separation and loss, sadistic and
      demanding transference, 64–
      81
  see also persecutory anxieties
as-if quality, absent in transference,
      33
atonement: *see* reparation
attachment, as burden, 100–101

197